D1336677

700039427947

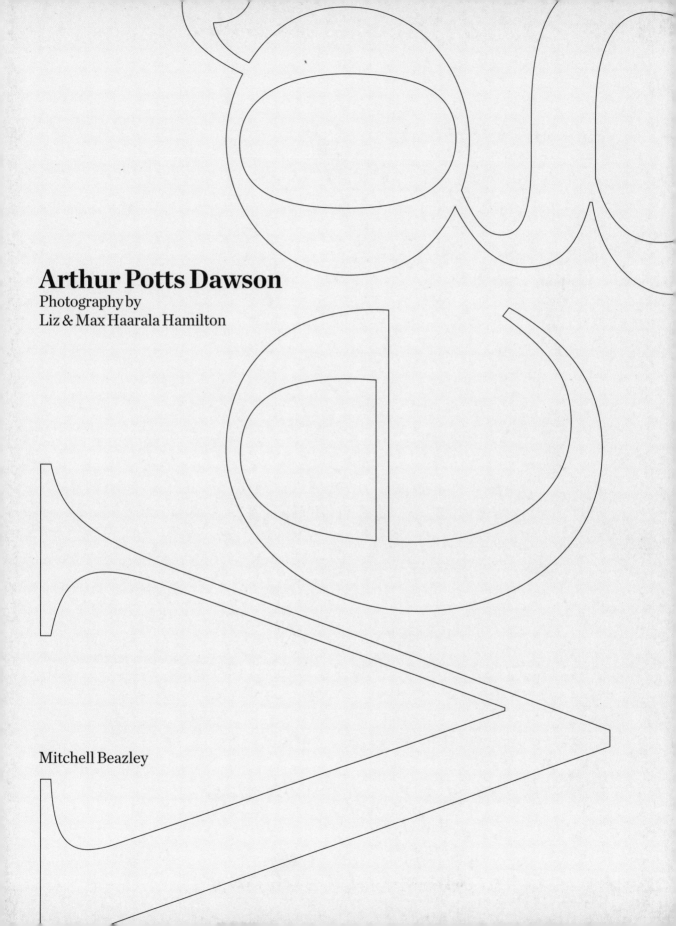

Arthur Potts Dawson

Photography by
Liz & Max Haarala Hamilton

Mitchell Beazley

For Rose Gray and Sue Miles –
I know you are making heaven
more delicious

First published in Great
Britain in 2012 by Mitchell
Beazley, an imprint of
Octopus Publishing Group
Limited, Endeavour House,
189 Shaftesbury Avenue,
London, WC2H 8JY

www.octopusbooks.co.uk

An Hachette UK Company
www.hachette.co.uk

Copyright © Octopus
Publishing Group Ltd 2012
Text copyright ©
Arthur Potts Dawson 2012
Photography copyright ©
Liz & Max Haraala
Hamilton 2012

The publishers will be
grateful for any information
that will assist them in
keeping future editions
up to date. Although all
reasonable care has been
taken in the preparation
of this book, neither the
publishers nor the author
can accept any liability for
any consequence arising
from the use thereof, or
the information contained
therein.

The author has asserted
his moral rights.

978-1-84533-659-2

A CIP record for this book
is available from the British
Library.

Set in Chronicle Deck.

Printed and bound in China.

Publishing Director:
Stephanie Jackson
Art Director:
Jonathan Christie
Design: Untitled
Photography: Liz & Max
Haraala Hamilton
Food styling:
Arthur Potts Dawson
Assistant Chef:
Robert Jagger
Production Manager:
Katherine Hockley
Editor: Jo Wilson
Copy Editor: Jo Richardson
Proofreader:
Patricia Burgess
Indexer: Hilary Bird

Note: Some recipes contain
nuts and nut derivatives.
Anyone with a known nut
allergy must avoid these.
This book contains
some dishes made with
raw or lightly cooked
eggs. It is prudent for more
vulnerable people such as
pregnant and nursing
mothers, invalids, the
elderly, babies and young
children, to avoid raw or
lightly cooked eggs.

Onions, garlic, fresh ginger
and vegetables should be
peeled or trimmed and
washed before use. Baby
root veg usually just require
washing.

All spoon measures are level.

All eggs are medium (size 3)
and free range.

Herbs are fresh unless stated
otherwise.

Contents

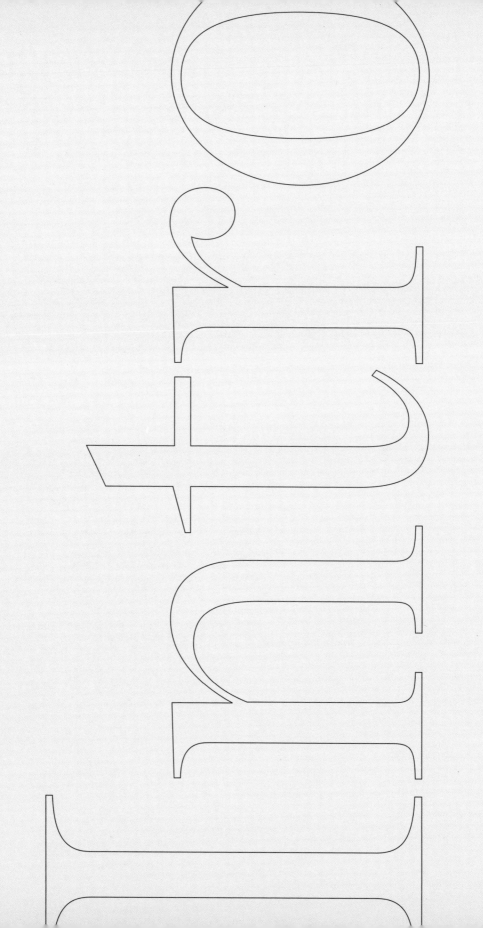

The more of the rainbow you eat, the better you'll feel

We all know we should eat more veg. We all know we should eat less meat. This book isn't a preach or a rant about why cooking and eating fresh, seasonal, local, organic food matters, though of course it does. I'm not going to tell you how to shop (locally, at the market, making the most of what's on special). I'm not even going to tell you to grow your own (go on – have a go!). *Eat Your Veg* is simply a storehouse of my favourite recipes encouraging you to do just that – eat more vegetables. It's a good, old-fashioned cookbook designed to help you make the most of our seasons and the different flavours created by the power of the sun. With over 250 recipes to dip into, arranged by vegetable, you just have to open it up and look at the amazing colours to see how these beauties deserve to be given far more prominence at our dining tables and on our plates.

For most of us, veggies are just the accompaniment: think of your Sunday roast, for example. You might decide on chicken or roast beef. But what about the roast potatoes and garlic cloves? The carrots, parsnips, mushrooms, tomatoes, onions, beetroot, asparagus, courgettes and other vegetables are the unsung heroes of cooking. We all need a little help to flip the way we cook, and this book shows you how to pull all of these delicious vegetables to the forefront. This isn't about becoming vegetarian, and this isn't a vegetarian cookbook – this is about putting veg at the centre of the plate. I'll show you hundreds of ways to prepare wicked-tasting dishes that do just fine with only a little fish and meat, or none at all.

After 25 years as a professional chef I know that the key to cooking veg is to use what's in season – it'll taste better, it'll cost you less, and the more of the rainbow you eat, the better you'll feel. So start with that – whether you're planning an evening meal or an entire feast based around vegetables. Next, choose your star vegetable and turn to the relevant section, where you will find a crop of hard-won and tried and tasted dishes. As well as individual recipes, I've created four gorgeous Feasts that, even if they contain a bit of meat or fish, show you really can create fantastic meals centred on vegetables. Elsewhere, to give you a handle on some good Skills, I've covered mashing, roasting, gratins, pickling and tomato sauce. With these under your belt you'll be able to cook tons of stuff with confidence and even create your own recipes and variations. And there are some handy Basics too at the back of the book.

With all of these vegetable-centred recipes, you will sail through the seasons, cooking lip-smackingly delicious meals, and you'll find it a breeze to adapt the methods to other vegetables, choose your own accompaniments and create your very own feasts.

I hope this book also goes some way to showing you how to lower your impact on the environment. Eating more veg, buying what's in season, buying fresh and locally, as well as growing your own, all contribute to your health – and the health of our precious home.

Given what's available every day in the supermarket, it's easy to lose sight of what's in season when. Here's a reminder of when you can enjoy different vegetables at their peak.

What's Best When?

Spring

Artichoke (globe, Jerusalem), asparagus, avocado, beans (broad, French), beetroot, french beans, broccoli (purple sprouting), cabbage, carrot, cucumber, cauliflower, celeriac, celery, chard, chicory, kale, leek, lettuce, mushroom, onion, parsnip, pea, potato, pumpkin, radish, spinach, spring greens, spring onion, stinging nettle, swede, turnip, tomato, samphire, sorrel, sugarsnap pea, watercress

Summer

Artichoke (globe), asparagus, aubergine, beans (borlotti, broad), beetroot, broccoli, cabbage, carrot, cauliflower, celery, chicory, chillies, courgette, cucumber, fennel, garlic, lettuce, mangetout, pea, potato (new), radish, rocket, samphire, shallot, sorrel, spinach, spring onion, squash, sugarsnap, sweetcorn, sweet pepper, tomato

Autumn

Artichoke (globe, Jerusalem), aubergine, beetroot, Brussels sprout, broccoli, borlotti bean, cabbage, carrot, cauliflower, celeriac, celery, chard, chicory, courgette, cucumber, fennel, garlic, kale, leek, lettuce, mushrooms, parsnip, pea, potato (new), radish, rocket, salsify, samphire, shallot, sorrel, spinach, spring onion, squash and pumpkin, swede, sweet pepper, sweet potato, sweetcorn, tomato, turnip, watercress

Winter

Artichoke (Jerusalem), beetroot, Brussels sprout, broccoli, cabbage, carrot, celeriac, celery, chard, kale, leek, okra, parsnips, pea, potato, radicchio, salsify, samphire, shallot, spinach, spring onion, squash and pumpkin, stinging nettle, swede, turnip

The Eat Your Veg Larder

If you keep a few key ingredients to hand, you'll be able to create delicious veg dishes all the time. Here are some of the things that I like to keep in stock in the fridge, freezer and storecupboard.

Herbs Basil, bay, chervil, chives, coriander, dill, flat leaf parsley, Indian bay leaves, lemon thyme, marjoram, mint, oregano, parsley, rosemary, saffron, sage, tarragon, thyme

Spices Allspice berries, caraway seeds, celery salt, Chinese five spice, cinnamon (ground, sticks), cumin (ground, seeds), curry powder, dried red chilli flakes, ground coriander, fennel seeds, fleur de sel, fresh root ginger, garam masala, juniper berries, paprika, peppercorns, rock salt, sea salt, smoked paprika, star anise, turmeric, white peppercorns, whole nutmeg, yellow mustard seeds

Dried fruits & veg Apricots, cranberries, raisins, sun-dried tomatoes, black-eyed peas, chickpeas, red lentils, Puy lentils, dried mushrooms (shiitake, porcini), capers

Vinegars & oils White wine vinegar, herb vinegar, cider vinegar, balsamic vinegar; light olive oil, extra virgin olive oil, sesame oil, sunflower oil, vegetable oil

Nuts & seeds Almonds, cashews, peanuts, pine nuts, pistachio nuts, pumpkin seeds, sesame seeds, sunflower seeds, walnuts

Dried pasta & grains Durum wheat lasagne, penne, spaghetti, couscous, polenta, quinoa, rice (arborio, basmati, white long-grain), Thai rice noodles

Condiments Chilli sauce, clear honey, coconut milk, mirin (rice wine), miso paste, mustard, olives, soy sauce, Thai fish sauce, wasabi paste, white wine, Worcestershire sauce, tahini paste, tamarind paste, tomato purée

Dairy Butter (lightly salted), Cheese (Cheddar, Gran padano or mild cheddar, goats' cheese, gruyère, haloumi, mozzarella, Parmesan, pecorino, ricotta, Stilton), crème fraîche, double cream, fresh free-range eggs, soured cream, yoghurt

Freezer Homemade breadcrumbs, pastry (filo, puff), stock

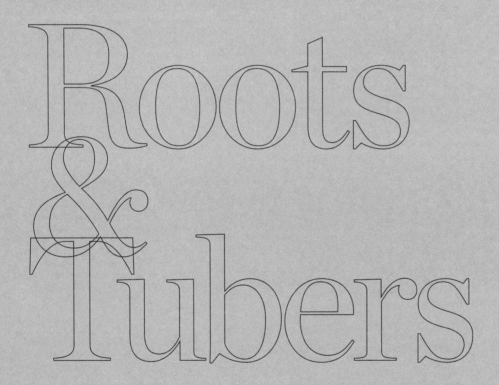

Roots & Tubers

Every time I put this soup in front of someone, their reaction to the colour is brilliant. It's not just the sight that dazzles, though – the flavours are even bigger than the colours, and the texture is just so smooth.

Beetroot soup with cumin & coriander

- 2kg (4lb 8oz) whole red beetroot, topped and tailed
- 1 large red onion
- 1 head of celery
- 100ml (3½fl oz) olive oil
- 3 garlic cloves, finely chopped
- 1 tsp cumin seeds
- 1 tsp dried red chilli flakes
- 50ml (2fl oz) red wine vinegar
- 350ml (12fl oz) vodka
- 2 litres (3½ pints) Vegetable stock (*see* page 297)
- 350ml (12fl oz) crème fraîche, plus extra to garnish
- 2 tbsp chopped coriander
- small beetroot leaves, to garnish
- salt and pepper

Serves 4–6 | Vegetarian

1   Cut the the beetroot into cubes about 4–5cm (1½–2in). I find that if you keep the pieces chunky, the soup ends up creamier. Cut the red onion into similar-sized pieces, then trim the celery and do the same with that.

2   Heat the olive oil in a large saucepan. Add the beetroot, onion, celery and garlic and cook over a medium heat for 10 minutes, stirring occasionally. Add the cumin seeds, chilli flakes and some salt and pepper, then cook for a further 10 minutes, or until the vegetables begin to soften and catch on the base of the pan.

3   Add the vinegar and vodka, stirring to loosen any browned bits on the base, then allow all the liquid to evaporate before adding the stock. Bring to the boil, then reduce the heat and simmer, uncovered, for at least 1 hour, or until the beetroot is tender when pierced with a knife.

4   Add the crème fraîche and coriander, then transfer to a blender in batches and blend until smooth. Check the seasoning and serve hot or cold in soup bowls, with an extra touch of crème fraîche spooned into the centre and topped with a small beetroot leaf.

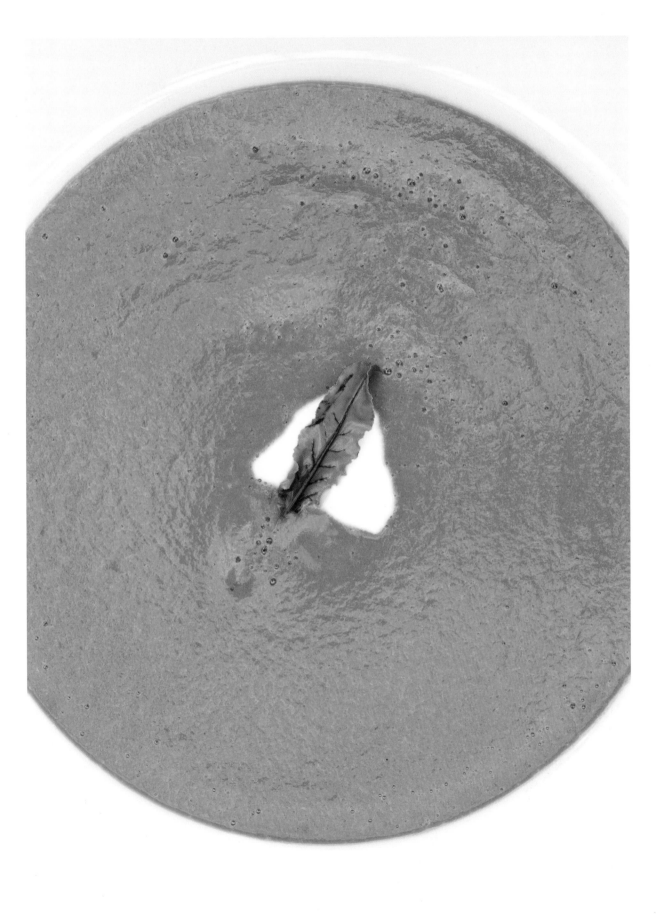

Beetroot is superb with watercress or horseradish, but the combination of the three takes this salad to a new level. I love the fire of the horseradish and the peppery taste of the watercress with the sweet root.

Beetroot salad with watercress & horseradish

- 1kg (2lb 4oz) whole red beetroot, topped and tailed
- olive oil, for drizzling
- 2 bunches of watercress, separated into sprigs
- 100g (3½oz) fresh horseradish root
- salt and pepper

Dressing
- 100ml (3½fl oz) clear honey
- 2 tbsp red wine vinegar
- 55g (2oz) Dijon mustard
- 125ml (4fl oz) olive oil
- salt and pepper

Serves 4–6 | Vegetarian

1   Preheat the oven to 180°C/fan 160°C/gas mark 4. Put the beetroot on a roasting tray, drizzle with olive oil and season with salt and pepper. Roast for about 1½ hours – depending on the size of the beetroots – or until a knife goes through them without any resistance but they are still slightly firm. Leave until cool enough to handle.

2   Put all the dressing ingredients into a clean screw-top jar, secure the lid and go crazy with the shaking. Give it a really good mix, and then create your salad.

3   Slice the roasted beetroot into discs 2cm (¾in) thick. Arrange them on serving plates and sprinkle over the watercress. Peel the horseradish and finely grate over the top of the salad. Spoon over the dressing to finish.

Beurre blanc and smoked eel is a classic combination. The beetroot brightens it up and takes it to a new level. This combination is, for me, a new classic.

Warm beetroot with smoked eel & beurre rouge

- 1kg (2lb 4oz) whole red beetroot, topped and tailed
- 600 g (1lb 5 oz) smoked eel fillets
- 1 handful of celery leaves

Beurre rouge
- 4 small shallots, thinly sliced
- 1 red beetroot, topped and tailed and cut into 3cm (1¼in) cubes
- pinch of salt
- 1 tsp whole black peppercorns
- 100ml (3½fl oz) red wine vinegar
- 200ml (7fl oz) red wine
- 50ml (2fl oz) double cream
- 225g (8oz) cold butter, cut into small cubes

Serves 4–6

1   Put the whole beetroot into a large saucepan. Cover well with cold water, add a generous sprinkling of salt and bring to the boil. Cover the pan and continue cooking for about 1 hour – depending on the size of the beetroot – or until a knife goes through them without any resistance but they are still slightly firm. Check and top up the water if necessary.

2   Meanwhile, for the beurre rouge, put the shallots and beetroot cubes into a small, heavy-based saucepan with the salt, peppercorns, vinegar and wine. Bring to the boil, reduce the heat and simmer for 20 minutes, or until the liquid has reduced to about 2 tablespoons with the consistency of honey. Bring to the boil, stir in the cream, then reduce the heat.

3   With the beurre rouge over a low heat, use a balloon whisk to mix in the butter one cube at a time, waiting for each piece to emulsify with the sauce before dropping in the next. Once you have a good emulsion, you can add the butter slightly more quickly. Continue whisking until smooth. Strain it through a fine sieve into a clean saucepan and keep warm, but don't return it to the direct heat or the butter will separate from the other liquids.

4   Once the whole beetroot is cooked, drain and leave until cool enough to handle. Preheat the oven to 190°C/fan 170°C/gas mark 5. Lay the eel fillets on a baking sheet and warm in oven for 5 minutes.

5   Cut the whole warm beetroot into pieces about 6 x 2.5cm (2½x 1in). Peel away and discard the skin from the eel , then pull each fillet into quarters. Arrange the celery leaves on serving plates and add the beetroot pieces, followed by the eel, then drizzle the beurre rouge on top.

This is a superfood salad, full of vitamins and minerals – great for picnics and summer lunches outdoors. You really don't need to eat meat with this salad; it has everything you need. This is a very pretty dish, and it tastes good too.

Raw beetroot salad with pumpkin & sunflower seeds

- 600g (1lb 5oz) red beetroot
- 600g (1lb 5oz) carrots
- 300g (10½oz) fennel bulb
- juice of 1 large lemon
- 3 tbsp pumpkin seeds
- 2 tbsp sunflower seeds
- 2 tsp sesame seeds
- 100g (3½oz) wild rocket
- 200ml (7fl oz) olive oil
- 100ml (3½fl oz) balsamic vinegar
- salt and pepper

Serves 4–6 | Vegetarian

1   Top and tail the beetroot and carrots, then peel only the carrots. Cut off the top of the fennel and trim off any outer tough leaves. Coarsely grate all three vegetables into a large bowl. Add the lemon juice and season with salt and pepper. Mix well with a metal spoon. The ingredients will all start to turn purple, but don't worry, as the salad will still retain the distinct flavours and textures of the carrot and fennel.

2   Heat a dry frying pan over a medium-high heat, tip in the seeds and mix and shake them in the pan until they start to crackle and toast. Once they are lightly browned, tip the seeds out onto a plate. Mix half of them in a bowl with the rocket and pour in the olive oil. Combine with the grated vegetables.

3   Arrange the salad on serving plates, topping each with the remaining toasted seeds and a drizzle of balsamic vinegar.

This is a lovely dish and one that my aunt Lilly in Norway cooked for me on one of my visits to Oslo. If you can't find rollmops, use good smoked mackerel instead. I've used golden beetroot in this recipe, but red beetroot will still look brilliant and they are cooked the same way. If you do use red beetroot, though, try not to mix it into the salad too soon, or it will bleed its colour into the dish.

Scandinavian beetroot with soused herrings & potato

- **12 rollmop herrings**
- **500g (1lb 2oz) cooked waxy potatoes, cut into 3cm (1¼in) cubes**
- **1 large Bramley apple, cored and cut into 3cm (1¼in) cubes**
- **500g (1lb 2oz) cooked golden beetroot, cut into 3cm (1¼in) cubes**
- **3 free-range eggs**
- **1 white onion, very thinly sliced into rings**
- **dried red chilli flakes, to garnish**

Dressing
- **3 tbsp wholegrain mustard**
- **3 tbsp caster sugar**
- **2 tbsp herb vinegar**
- **3 tsp chopped dill, plus extra sprigs to garnish**
- **500ml (18fl oz) double cream**
- **salt and pepper**

Serves 4–6

1   Unroll the rollmop fillets and cut them in half lengthways. Put the potato, apple and beetroot into a serving bowl and mix well.

2   Bring a saucepan of water to the boil, carefully add the eggs and cook for 8 minutes. Remove the pan from the heat and place it under a slow-running cold tap until the pan turns cold. Drain the eggs, then shell and cut into quarters.

3   For the dressing, put the mustard, sugar, vinegar, chopped dill and salt and pepper into a small mixing bowl and whisk together until well combined. In a separate mixing bowl, whip the cream until it forms soft ribbons when you let it fall from the whisk, then pour in the vinegar mixture and whisk to combine.

4   Divide the salad mixture between serving plates and drizzle the dressing over the salad. Arrange the rollmop fillets on top, followed by the onion rings and egg quarters. Finish this dish with a small scattering of chilli flakes and then some dill sprigs.

Warming, spicy, tangy and fresh, this soup rocks every time I taste it. Increase the chilli if you like – the flavours will get even more fantastic.

Carrot & ginger soup

- 75ml (2¹/₂fl oz) olive oil
- 1 large white onion, cut into 2cm (³/₄in) cubes
- 1 head of celery, trimmed and cut into 2cm (³/₄in) cubes
- 2kg (4lb 8oz) carrots, cut into 2cm (³/₄in) cubes
- 3 garlic cloves
- 25g (1oz) fresh root ginger, peeled and cut into 1cm (¹/₂in) cubes
- 1 tsp dried red chilli flakes
- 100g (3¹/₂oz) white long-grain rice
- 200ml (7fl oz) medium-dry white wine
- 2 litres (3¹/₂ pints) Vegetable stock (*see* page 297)
- 200ml (7fl oz) milk
- 1 tsp freshly grated nutmeg
- juice of 1 lemon
- salt and pepper

To garnish
- crème fraîche
- coriander leaves

Serves 4–6 | Vegetarian

1 Heat the olive oil in a large saucepan, add the onion and celery and cook over a medium heat for 5 minutes, stirring occasionally. Add the carrots, the whole garlic cloves and ginger, then season with salt and pepper and add the chilli flakes. Cook for 15 minutes, stirring occasionally so that the vegetables don't stick to the base of the pan. Add the rice and cook for a further 5 minutes, stirring frequently.

2 Add the wine to the pan, stirring to loosen any browned bits on the base, then allow all the liquid to evaporate before adding the stock. Bring to the boil, then reduce the heat and simmer, uncovered, for 20 minutes, or until the rice is tender.

3 Add the milk and nutmeg and allow the soup to come almost to boiling point before turning off the heat. Leave to cool for a few minutes, then transfer to a blender in batches and blend until smooth. Return all the soup to the pan, add the lemon juice and check the seasoning, then reheat gently. Pour the soup into bowls, add a spoonful of crème fraîche to the centre of each and surround with a few coriander leaves.

This is the type of dish I cook at home all the time. There is something about butter and soy sauce that really works together. Scrubbing rather than peeling the baby carrots keeps their full flavour and goodness.

Baby carrots with butter & soy

- 2 bunches of baby carrots
- 200g (7oz) butter
- 2 tbsp olive oil
- 50ml (2fl oz) light soy sauce
- salt and pepper
- snipped chives, to garnish

Serves 4 | Vegetarian

1   Top and tail the carrots, and scrub rather than peel them. Put them into a saucepan, cover well with cold water and add a little salt. Bring to the boil, then reduce the heat and simmer for 5–8 minutes, or until cooked but not soft.

2   Drain the carrots in a colander and return them to the pan. Add the butter, olive oil and soy sauce, season with salt and pepper and roll the carrots in the mixture. Serve straight away, scattered with some snipped chives.

Jerusalem artichokes with butter & soy

Try using Jerusalem artichokes in place of the carrots for this simple dish. Peel 500g (1lb 2oz) Jerusalem artichokes and discard the trimmings. Cut and cook them as for the carrots above. The soy sauce leaves a lovely colour in the white flesh.

In the old French kitchens I used to work in, Vichy water was imported specifically for this dish. The minerals in the water add a depth I still don't truly understand. Use another mineral water if you can't get Vichy, but if neither is available, this dish is still delicious.

Spring carrots à la Vichy

- 8 large carrots
- 2.5 litres (2¾ pints) sparkling Vichy mineral water
- 150g (5½oz) butter
- salt and pepper
- flat leaf parsley sprig, to garnish

Serves 4 | Vegetarian

1   Top and tail the carrots, and scrub rather than peel them. Cut them into discs 2cm (¾in) thick and put them into a heavy-based saucepan.

2   Just cover with the sparkling mineral water and add the butter, salt and pepper. Place the pan over a medium-high heat and cook for 20 minutes, by which time the water will have evaporated and left behind a buttery sauce. Stir once during cooking. Serve with a flat leaf parsley sprig.

This dish is deep and sensuous. The horseradish loses its heat but changes into the most delicious parsnipy-flavoured root vegetable I have ever tasted.

Carrot & horseradish stew with oxtail & red wine

- 2kg (4lb 8oz) large pieces of oxtail
- 2 tbsp plain flour
- 100ml (3¹/2fl oz) olive oil
- 50g (1³/4oz) butter
- 8 large carrots, cut into discs 4cm (1¹/2in) thick
- 6 rashers of streaky bacon, cut into 2cm (³/4in) pieces
- 1 large white onion, cut into 2cm (³/4in) cubes
- 1 large fresh horseradish root, cut into 4cm (1¹/2in) discs
- 6 garlic cloves
- 75cl bottle good red wine
- 3 large tomatoes, chopped
- 2 tbsp tomato purée
- 1 litre (1³/4 pints) Vegetable stock (*see* page 297)
- 500ml (18fl oz) Chicken stock (*see* page 297)
- 1 bouquet garni of thyme, rosemary, parsley and bay leaves, tied together with string
- salt and pepper

Serves 4–6

1   Prepare the oxtail by cutting off any fatty-looking pieces and dab off any moisture with kitchen paper. Season the flour with salt and pepper, then roll the oxtail pieces in it.

2   Heat the olive oil in a flameproof casserole dish with a tight-fitting lid and fry the oxtail in 2 batches over a medium-high heat until golden brown all over – about 10 minutes. Transfer to a colander.

3   Tip out the pan juices and add the butter, stirring, to loosen any brown bits from the base of the pan. When the butter has melted, add the carrot, bacon, onion, horseradish and whole garlic cloves and cook over a medium heat for 5 minutes, stirring occasionally.

4   Return the oxtail to the pan, increase the heat and once everything is hot, add the wine and cook, stirring occasionally for 20 minutes. Add the tomatoes, tomato purée and the stocks and season well with salt and pepper. Lower in the bouquet garni and lay a sheet of greaseproof paper over the whole pan. Put the pan lid on, then reduce the heat to low and cook for 3 hours, stirring occasionally, until all the liquid has evaporated. Check the meat to make sure it is falling off the bone before serving.

In umido roughly translates from Italian as 'in humid conditions'. The trick to creating these conditions is to use a high-sided saucepan to keep the steam inside while you braise the vegetables. The flavours really come together with this style of cooking.

Carrots, broad beans & peas in umido

- 600g (1lb 5oz) carrots, trimmed and scrubbed
- 600g (1lb 5oz) young peas in their pods
- 600g (1lb 5oz) young broad beans in their pods
- 1 bunch of spring onions
- 3 celery sticks
- 150ml (¼ pint) olive oil
- 2 garlic cloves
- 150ml (¼ pint) medium-dry white wine
- 500ml (18fl oz) Vegetable stock (*see* page 297)
- salt and pepper

Serves 4–6 | Vegetarian

1   Cut the carrots into irregular shapes the size of a large marble. Put them into a saucepan, cover well with cold water and add a little salt. Bring to the boil, then reduce the heat and simmer for 12 minutes.

2   Meanwhile, pod the peas and broad beans. Trim and chop the spring onions and celery to match the size of the peas. Heat the olive oil in a high-sided saucepan, add the spring onion and celery and cook over a medium-high heat for 5 minutes, until golden brown, stirring frequently. Chop the garlic finely, add to the onion mixture and cook, stirring, for 2 minutes. Add the peas and broad beans and cook for a further 2 minutes, stirring frequently. Add the wine and allow all the liquid to evaporate, about 6 minutes, before adding the stock and bringing to the boil.

3   Drain the carrots and add them to the pan of vegetables. Cook until the stock has evaporated to leave only a little, then season well with salt and pepper and serve warm.

Yellow wax beans in umido with tomatoes & basil

- 650g (1lb 7oz) yellow wax beans or green beans, topped and tailed
- 75ml (2½fl oz) olive oil, plus extra for drizzling
- 2 garlic cloves, thinly sliced
- 1 tsp finely chopped basil leaves
- 400g (14oz) large tomatoes, cut into 1cm (½in) dice
- salt and pepper

Serves 4–6 | Vegetarian

1   Put the yellow wax beans into a saucepan of salted boiling water and cook for 4 minutes. Drain and set aside.

2   Heat the olive oil in a high-sided frying pan, add the garlic and cook over a medium heat for 5 minutes, until lightly coloured, stirring occasionally. Add the basil and cook, stirring, for 2 minutes. Add the tomatoes, season with salt and pepper and leave to cook for 20 minutes, stirring occasionally. Stir in the cooked beans and cook for a further 15 minutes.

3   Drizzle in a little more olive oil and check the seasoning. Serve warm or at room temperature.

You need to leave this dish to marinate for at least an hour. Use the biggest holes on the grater so that the carrots keep their crunch.

Carrot salad with raisins, pistachios & mint

- 1.2kg (2lb 10oz) carrots
- 300g (10½oz) raisins
- 3 tbsp chopped mint
- 100ml (3½fl oz) mirin (rice wine)
- 50ml (2fl oz) light soy sauce
- 150g (5½oz) raw unsalted pistachio nuts, shelled
- pepper

Serves 4–6 | Vegetarian

1   Coarsely grate the carrots into a mixing bowl. Add the raisins, mint, mirin, soy sauce and pepper. Mix well, cover the bowl with clingfilm and leave at room temperature for 1 hour for the flavours to develop.

2   Meanwhile, heat a dry frying pan over a medium-high heat, tip in the pistachios and lightly toast them for a couple of minutes, shaking the pan often. Watch them carefully and remove from the heat before they burn. Leave to cool.

3   Mix the toasted pistachios through the salad and serve.

Pass this parsnip soup through a fine sieve to make the silkiest soup this side of the Milky Way.

Parsnip & lemon soup

- 2kg (4lb 8oz) parsnips
- 1 large white onion
- 1 celery heart
- 3 garlic cloves
- 150g (5½oz) butter
- juice and finely grated rind of 2 unwaxed lemons, plus extra juice to taste
- 250ml (9fl oz) medium-dry white wine
- 2 litres (3½ pints) Vegetable stock (*see* page 297)
- 250ml (9fl oz) milk
- salt and pepper
- lemon slices, peeled, to garnish

Serves 4–6 | Vegetarian

1   Cut the parsnips, onion and celery heart into 2cm (3/4in) cubes. Roughly chop the garlic cloves.

2   Melt the butter in a heavy-based saucepan, add all the vegetables and the garlic, season with salt and pepper and mix well. Cook over a medium heat for 15 minutes, stirring occasionally. Add the juice and lemon rind and the wine and allow the liquid to evaporate before adding the stock. Bring to the boil, then reduce the heat and simmer for 20 minutes, until the parsnips are tender.

3   Add the milk and allow the soup to come almost to boiling point before turning off the heat. Leave to cool for a few minutes, then transfer to a blender in batches and blend until smooth, or keep it whole and chunky – either way, the flavour will be amazing. Add a touch more lemon juice if you don't think the soup is lemony enough, and check the seasoning. Return to the pan to reheat gently, if blended. Serve warm, in bowls, with a slice of peeled lemon placed in the centre.

I thought of creating this salad because both the parsnips and shiitakes have a creamy finish. Add a little soy and mirin and – wow!

Parsnip & shiitake salad

- 1kg (2lb 4oz) parsnips
- 600g (1lb 5oz) dried shiitake mushrooms, soaked in hot water to rehydrate until the water is cold
- 300g (10^{1}/$_{2}$oz) girolle mushrooms
- 100ml (3^{1}/$_{2}$fl oz) mirin (rice wine)
- 75ml (2^{1}/$_{2}$fl oz) rice wine vinegar
- 75ml (2^{1}/$_{2}$fl oz) sesame oil
- 50ml (2fl oz) brown miso paste
- 2 shallots, finely chopped
- 50ml (2fl oz) light soy sauce
- 4 tbsp chopped chervil
- salt

Serves 4–6 | Vegetarian

1   Cut the parsnips lengthways into thirds. Put them into a saucepan, cover well with cold water and add a pinch of salt. Bring to the boil, then reduce the heat to a gentle roll and cook for 15 minutes, or until tender but not too soft – you don't want them falling apart in the salad. Drain in a colander, transfer to a large bowl and set aside.

2   Drain the shiitake mushrooms and trim off any remaining hard bits – check the stalks especially. Gently brush any dirt off the girolle mushrooms and add both the shiitake and girolle mushrooms to the parsnips.

3   Put the mirin, vinegar, sesame oil, miso paste, shallots and soy sauce into a small mixing bowl and whisk together. Pour over the parsnip mixture and gently toss in the bowl. Serve on individual plates and sprinkle with the chopped chervil.

Honey, mustard and the creamy texture of the parsnips is a classic combination. I love the way the ingredients turn a dark golden colour, with some of the edges just on their way to lightly burning. This is a dish of sticky, tangy loveliness.

Honey-mustard parsnips

- 1.5kg (3lb 5oz) parsnips
- 200ml (7fl oz) clear honey
- 3 tbsp wholegrain mustard
- 3 tbsp thyme leaves
- 150ml (¼ pint) olive oil
- finely grated rind of 2 oranges
- salt and pepper

Serves 4–6 | Vegetarian

1 Preheat the oven to 180°C/fan 160°C/gas mark 4. Cut the parsnips lengthways into sixths. Put them into a saucepan, cover well with cold water and add a pinch of salt. Bring to the boil, then drain in a colander and transfer to a large bowl.

2 While the parsnips are still hot and steamy, add all the remaining ingredients, season with salt and pepper and mix well. Spread the mixture out on a roasting tray, and roast for 10 minutes, until the edges and tips of the parsnips are golden brown.

Honey-mustard carrots

If you're looking for another partner for a roast, you could try substituting the parsnips with carrots. Scrub 1.5kg (3lb 5oz) carrots and prepare them like the parsnips above. Add 4 tsp sweet chilli sauce to the mix in the tray for a piquant finish.

This has to be the easiest soup to make in the world. You can use pretty much any mushroom you like – button, chestnut, flat cap – but I use the wild morels that arrive at the beginning of the main mushroom season in autumn. They're wonderfully earthy, subtly flavoured and brilliantly textured.

Potato & morel soup

- 2kg (4lb 8oz) King Edward or other floury potatoes
- 1 garlic clove
- leaves from 2 thyme sprigs
- 500g (1lb 2oz) morel mushrooms
- 200ml (7fl oz) single cream
- 200ml (7fl oz) double cream
- extra virgin olive oil, for drizzling
- salt and pepper

Serves 4–6 | Vegetarian

1   Cut the potatoes in half, rinse thoroughly and put them in a large saucepan. Cover well with cold water and add the whole garlic clove, thyme leaves and a pinch of salt. Bring to the boil, then reduce the heat. Skim off any white foam that rises to the surface and simmer for about 35 minutes, or until a knife goes through the potatoes without any resistance but they are still slightly firm.

2   While the potatoes are cooking, clean the mushrooms really well with a small brush, then chop them roughly. Once the potatoes are done, drain them and return to the pan. Add the mushrooms, then mash up the mixture until the potatoes and mushrooms are combined. Add the creams then give the mixture a really good whisk with a balloon whisk. The more vigorous you are at this stage, the smoother the soup is going to be, but I like to keep it slightly chunky. Grind in some pepper and check the salt.

3   Serve the soup straight away, with a drizzle of extra virgin olive oil. I like to serve it hot, but bear in mind that this is basically liquid mashed potato and stays really hot, so be careful!

For as long as I can remember, mashed potato has been in my life, from lumpy and cold in primary school, through fluffy and buttery at my grandmother's to smooth and silky in top restaurants. It's safe to say I love mash and, what's more, it's a universally pleasing dish that everyone should have in their repertoire. Start with this recipe, then try the others overleaf once you've mastered it. This particular variety of mash, with its subtle garlic flavours and punchy rosemary, goes brilliantly with roast lamb. But sometimes the best way to enjoy it is on its own.

My favourite mash

- 2kg (4lb 8oz) King Edward or other floury potatoes
- 3 garlic cloves
- 300ml (1/2 pint) milk
- 200g (7oz) butter
- 1 small bunch of rosemary
- whole nutmeg, for grating
- sea salt and pepper

Serves 4–6 | Vegetarian

1   Cut the potatoes into large chunks – too small and they will absorb too much water, but too big and the outside will cook before the middle. 6–7cm (2^1/$_2$–2^3/$_4$in) is about right.

2   Rinse the potatoes thoroughly and put them into a large saucepan. Cover well with cold water, add 2 good pinches of salt and the whole garlic cloves. Bring to the boil, then reduce the heat, skim off any white foam that rises to the surface and simmer for 30–35 minutes, or until a knife goes through the potatoes without any resistance but they are still slightly firm. Drain in a colander, allowing the steam to rise and the potatoes to dry, which helps to make the mash fluffy. Reserve the garlic cloves.

3   While the potatoes are drying, put the milk and butter into the empty saucepan with the rosemary and the reserved garlic cloves, and heat over a low heat until the butter has melted. Remove from the heat, season lightly with salt and pepper and grate in a couple of strokes of nutmeg.

4   Remove the rosemary sprigs, and pass the potatoes through a potato ricer or mouli set directly over the milk mixture. Alternatively, drop the potatoes into the milk mixture and mash by hand with a potato masher – you might end up with a few lumps, but some people love them. Check the seasoning and be brave with the salt.

Just mash

- 2kg (4lb 8oz) King Edward
  or other floury potatoes
- 300ml (½ pint) milk
- 200g (7oz) butter
- whole nutmeg, for grating
- salt and pepper

Serves 4–6 | Vegetarian

1 If you prefer your mash unadorned, follow the method on page 34, but omit the garlic and the rosemary.

Potato & celeriac mash

- 1.5kg (3lb 5oz) King Edward
  or other floury potatoes
- 500g (1lb 2oz) celeriac
- 3 garlic cloves
- 300ml (½ pint) milk
- 200g (7oz) butter
- 2 tsp finely chopped rosemary
- whole nutmeg, for grating
- celery salt

Serves 4–6 | Vegetarian

1 Follow the method on page 34, cooking the celeriac in the same way as the potatoes.

2 When seasoning at the end, use plenty of celery salt instead of ordinary salt.

Saffron & shallot mash

- 2kg (4lb 8oz) King Edward
  or other floury potatoes
- 3 garlic cloves
- 300ml (½ pint) milk
- 200g (7oz) butter
- 2 banana shallots, finely chopped
- 2 pinches of saffron threads
- whole nutmeg, for grating
- salt and pepper

Serves 4–6 | Vegetarian

1 Follow steps 1 and 2 on page 34. When you are warming the milk, butter, rosemary and garlic, add the shallots and saffron too. Saffron leaves an amazing flavour in the milk when heated up, and infuses the whole dish with a powerful aroma and yellow colour. Continue with steps 3 and 4. Serve with scallops, prawns or some poached smoked haddock.

Chervil, parsley & dill mash

- 2kg (4lb 8oz) King Edward
  or other floury potatoes
- 3 garlic cloves
- 300ml (½ pint) milk
- 200g (7oz) butter
- 2 tsp finely chopped rosemary
- whole nutmeg, for grating
- 6 tbsp finely chopped chervil
- 6 tbsp finely chopped parsley
- 6 tbsp finely chopped dill
- salt and pepper

Serves 4–6 | Vegetarian

1 Follow the method on page 34, adding the herbs at the last moment and stirring them through the mash.

Buttered mashed swede

- 1kg (2lb 4oz) swede, cut into 6–7cm
  (2½–2¾in) chunks
- 175g (6oz) butter, cut into small cubes
- salt and pepper

Serves 4–6 | Vegetarian

1 Put the swede into a saucepan, cover well with cold water and add 2 good pinches of salt. Bring to the boil, then reduce the heat and simmer for 35–40 minutes, or until tender but not mushy.

2 Drain in a colander and leave to allow the steam to rise and the swede to dry off slightly. Mash with a potato masher, adding the cubes of butter a few at a time. Season to taste – don't be shy with the pepper, or the salt for that matter. This is brilliant with some roast lamb.

Burns night neeps & tatties

Tatties
- 750g (1lb 10oz) King Edward potatoes
  cut into 6–7cm (2½–2¾in) chunks
- 125ml (4fl oz) milk
- 150g (5½oz) butter
- whole nutmeg, for grating
- salt and pepper

Neeps
- 750g (1lb 10oz) turnip or swede, cut into
  3cm (1¼in) cubes
- 150g (5½oz) butter
- 25g (1oz) fresh root ginger
  and finely chopped
- salt and pepper

Serves 4 | Vegetarian

1 Follow the method on page 34 for the tatties, but season with pepper as well as salt.

2 Meanwhile, for the neeps, put the turnips or swede into a saucepan, cover well with cold water and add the salt. Bring to the boil, then reduce the heat and simmer for 35–40 minutes, or until tender but not mushy. Drain in a colander, then return to the pan. Set over a medium heat for a further 5 minutes to allow any water to evaporate. Add the butter, ginger and lots of freshly ground pepper and mix well.

3 Serve the neeps & tatties alongside each other on the plate, with a hot haggis on the side if you wish.

Sometimes, for a change, I add sweet potato to this recipe, but you could use carrots, parsnips – hey, why not try a whole heap of different vegetables? The cooking method remains the same. The galette should be crunchy on the outside and soft in the middle, with a lovely sage flavour throughout.

Potato galettes with sage

- **6 large Maris Piper or other floury potatoes**
- **150ml (¼ pint) olive oil**
- **12 sage leaves, finely chopped**
- **150g (5½oz) butter**
- **salt and pepper**

Serves 8 | Vegetarian

1   Grate the potatoes coarsely. You need to work fairly fast because the potatoes will start to turn brown quite quickly and you can't rinse or store them in water, as you will wash away the starch needed to bind the galette.

2   Drizzle half the olive oil into a large frying pan and place over a medium heat without allowing it to get hot enough to smoke. Once you have grated half the potato, or enough to cover the base of the pan to a depth of 2cm (¾in), mix with half the chopped sage, and pat the potato down in the pan using a potato masher – this has a wide surface area and allows you to create a really even, flat pancake. Once the galette has begun to settle in the pan, start to add half the butter in very small pieces to the edges of the pan, letting it melt and run into the centre, which will give a lovely nutty flavour to the potatoes. Cook for 8–10 minutes, until golden brown on the underside. Gently slide the galette onto a wooden board, then place the pan over the galette and invert the board so the galette is back in the pan, cooked side up. Cook for 8–10 minutes, until the underside is golden brown and crunchy.

3   Remove the galette from the pan and keep warm while you grate and cook the remaining potato to make another galette. Serve the galettes hot, cut into wedges.

I lived in Spain for a couple of years, and every bar sells its own version of this classic dish. I defy you to resist nibbling the trimmed olive stones.

Russian salad

- 800g (1lb 12oz) salad potatoes, scrubbed, cooked whole and cooled
- 400g (14oz) French beans, topped and tailed, cut into 2cm (3/4in) lengths, cooked until slightly crunchy and cooled
- 400g (14oz) young carrots, scrubbed, cut into 2cm (3/4in) lengths, cooked until slightly crunchy and cooled
- 200g (7oz) frozen peas, cooked and refreshed in cold water
- 100g (3¹/2oz) capers in vinegar, drained and squeezed dry
- 200g (7oz) green olives, 3 sides cut off each
- 2 smoked chicken breasts, skinned and cut into 3cm (1¹/4in) cubes
- 3 tablespoons Homemade mayonnaise (*see* page 297)
- large outer leaves of 4 heads of Baby Gem lettuce
- 8 free-range eggs, hard-boiled and shelled
- salt and pepper
- chervil, dill or young flat leaf parsley sprigs, to garnish

Serves 4–6

1   Put the cooked potatoes, French beans, carrots, peas, capers, olives and smoked chicken into a large bowl. Add the mayonnaise and season with salt and pepper. Mix gently but thoroughly, until the ingredients are all covered with the mayonnaise.

2   Arrange the lettuce leaves around the edge of a large serving dish. Place the hard-boiled eggs on the leaves. Spoon the vegetable and chicken mixture into the middle of the plate. Garnish with the chervil, dill or parsley.

Your basic tortilla recipe can be varied, depending on the ingredients you have to hand. It's a great way to get kids to eat their greens. If you can't find any Padrón peppers, you can use ordinary green peppers and drop a crushed dried red chilli into the onion mixture.

Tortilla with Padrón peppers & paprika

- 2 large potatoes, cut into 3cm (1¼in) cubes
- 100ml (3½fl oz) olive oil
- 500g (1lb 2oz) green Padrón peppers, stalks trimmed
- 1 large white Spanish onion, cut into 2cm (¾in) cubes
- 1 garlic clove, finely chopped
- 1 tsp paprika
- 8 large free-range eggs
- salt and pepper

Serves 4–6 | Vegetarian

1   Put the potato cubes into a saucepan, cover well with cold water and add a little salt. Bring to the boil slowly to avoid breaking up the potatoes, then reduce the heat and simmer for 16–18 minutes, until tender but still with a bit of bite to them, as they will cook further in the tortilla. Drain well. Meanwhile, heat a little olive oil in a large frying pan and fry the Padrón peppers for 3 minutes. Remove from the pan while you make the tortilla.

2   Heat the remaining olive oil in a large frying pan, add the onion and cook over a gentle heat until translucent, stirring occasionally. Add the garlic and continue frying gently for 3 minutes. Add the paprika and the cooked potatoes. Increase the heat to medium-high and gently shake the pan and stir the mixture. Break the eggs into a bowl and give them a good whisk, seasoning with salt and pepper. Pour the eggs into the pan, then reduce the heat to medium. As the eggs begin to set, use a spatula to loosen the tortilla from the edge of the pan. Meanwhile, preheat the grill until very hot.

3   When the tortilla is nearly cooked, after about 4 minutes, transfer the pan to the grill (making sure that you turn the handle away from the heat source) – this will cook the top of the tortilla without you having to turn it over. Grill for about 6 minutes, until the whole tortilla is golden brown and firm, then give the pan a good shake to release it. To turn it out, place a wooden board on top of the pan and turn both the board and pan over at the same time. Serve the tortilla with the Padrón peppers and a glass of ice-cold Spanish beer.

Rocket & pea tortilla

- 500g (1lb 2oz) new potatoes
- 75ml (2½fl oz) olive oil
- 1 large white Spanish onion, cut into 2cm (¾in) cubes
- 1 garlic clove, chopped
- 1 tsp dried red chilli flakes
- 500g (1lb 2oz) fresh peas, podded
- 2 bunches of wild rocket
- 8 large free-range eggs
- salt and pepper

Serves 4–6 | Vegetarian

1   Scrub the potatoes and cut into quarters. Follow step 1 of the method above to boil and drain the potatoes. Follow step 2 to cook the onion and garlic. Add the chilli flakes and then the cooked potatoes to the pan, increase the heat to medium-high and gently shake the pan and stir the mixture as before. Add the peas and rocket and stir well. Continue as above with the eggs, then follow step 3.

These crunchy, chivey prawns make a lovely party plate. It's important to make the potato waistcoats thin so that they cook quickly and prevent the prawns overcooking.

Prawns in potato waistcoats

- 2 large potatoes
- 20g (³/₄oz) cornflour
- 3 tbsp cold water
- 4 tbsp finely chopped chives
- 24 large raw prawns, peeled but tails intact
- 50ml (2fl oz) olive oil
- 1 lemon
- salt and pepper

Serves 4–6

1   Trim the rounded sides off each potato so that you have 2 boxy shapes about 8cm (3¹/₄in) wide. Using a sharp knife, cut the blocks widthways into thin strips. You need to create 12 strips from each potato. Drop these into cold water.

2   Drain the potato strips and pat them dry. Soak 8 small wooden skewers in cold water. Mix the cornflour with the cold water to make a paste. Using a pastry brush, brush one side of each potato strip with the cornflour paste. Spread the chives out on a flat plate and season lightly with salt and pepper. Dip the prawns in the chives, then roll up each prawn in a potato strip, making sure they are completely enclosed. Take the wooden skewers out of the water and thread 3 prawns on to each.

3   Heat the olive oil in a frying pan, add the skewers and cook over a medium heat for 5–7 minutes, until a lovely golden brown, turning frequently to get an even colouring.

4   Serve with lemon cheeks, which have no pips, are super-easy to squeeze and leave most of the lemon intact for something else. Using a sharp knife, slice 6 pieces off the rounded sides of the lemon, each with a little of the flesh, as if you are making a similar shape to the potato. Also delicious with spicy mayonnaise (see page 297).

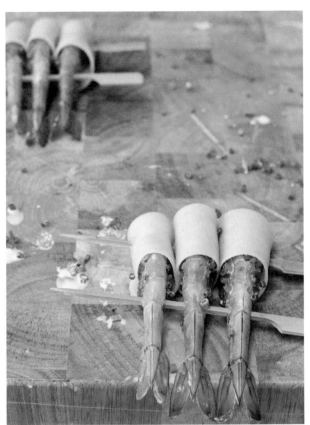

This classic, confit-style dish calls for lots of butter. The milk and saffron get absorbed by the potatoes to create the richest, most amazing flavour – creamy, caramelly and super-decadent. I think you should cook these potatoes every weekend.

Jersey Royal fondant potatoes with saffron

- 200g (7oz) butter
- 1kg (2lb 4oz) Jersey Royals, or other new potatoes
- milk, for covering the potatoes
- 4 bay leaves
- 1 pinch of saffron threads
- salt and pepper

Serves 4–6 | Vegetarian

1   Slice the butter evenly and lay it over the bottom of a heavy-based saucepan. Peel the potatoes, then rinse thoroughly and pat dry. Arrange the potatoes on the butter and pour enough milk into the pan to cover them. Add the bay leaves, sprinkle over the saffron threads and season with salt and pepper. Lay a circle of baking parchment on top and cook over a medium heat for 10 minutes. Remove the paper and continue to cook until the milk has evaporated – you will be left with a layer of butter, colouring the surface of the potatoes.

2   Turn off the heat and leave the potatoes to cool slightly for 5 minutes. Turn them over, return to the heat and cook for another 5 minutes until the other side of the fondant is coloured. Turn off the heat, wait for 2 minutes, then lift out the potatoes and serve hot.

This is so fresh and tasty. All the flavours get heated up by the baked potato, the juices come running out onto the plate, and mopping them up with the fluffy potato creates a lovely taste sensation.

Baked potatoes with tomatoes, basil & crème fraîche

- 12 small baking potatoes, scrubbed
- 800g (1lb 12oz) large ripe oxheart tomatoes, or any other large sweet variety, cut into small chunks
- 4 tbsp chopped basil, plus a few whole leaves, to garnish
- 200ml (7fl oz) olive oil
- 500ml (18fl oz) crème fraîche
- salt and pepper

Serves 6 | Vegetarian

1   Preheat the oven to 180°C/fan 160°C/gas mark 4. Put the potatoes in a baking tray and bake for 50–60 minutes, until soft.

2   Meanwhile, arrange the tomatoes on a large serving plate. Sprinkle half the basil over them, season with salt and pepper and drizzle over the olive oil. Leave to marinate at room temperature while the potatoes are baking.

3   When the potatoes are ready, split them open along their length and open them up by squeezing either side of the cut to push the potato flesh up and out of its skin. Place a teaspoonful of crème fraîche in each potato to begin with, then divide the tomatoes evenly over the top of them. Give the remaining crème fraîche a good stir, then drizzle all over the tops of the potatoes. Finish the dish by sprinkling over the rest of the basil.

The vinaigrette dressing I use here is a classic recipe I was given at the age of 16, using three parts olive oil, two parts vinegar and one part mustard. Serve in the sunshine, preferably on the Côte d'Azur with the Mediterranean twinkling and the yacht anchored in the distance, waiting for your return and the journey to Monte Carlo...

New potato salad niçoise

- 600g (1lb 5oz) new potatoes, scrubbed, cooked whole and cooled
- 300g (10½oz) ripe tomatoes, cut into small chunks
- 300g (10½oz) French beans, topped and tailed, cooked until slightly crunchy and cooled
- 3 free-range eggs, hard-boiled, shelled and halved
- 1 red pepper, cored, deseeded and cut into 4cm (1½in) pieces
- 2 shallots, thinly sliced
- 200g (7oz) can high-quality tuna, drained and flaked
- 100g (3½oz) salted anchovies, soaked in cold water for 30 minutes and drained
- 200g (7oz) Niçoise, or Taggiasca, olives
- 300ml (½pint) House dressing (*see* page 297)

Serves 4–6

1   Put all the ingredients in a bowl and gently combine, ensuring the dressing is mixed through. Alternatively, arrange the salad on serving plates, building up the ingredients, with the heaviest ingredients first – potatoes followed by tomatoes, beans, eggs, red pepper, shallots, tuna, anchovies and olives. Drizzle the whole salad with the dressing and serve.

Sprinkling the chilli and capers on to the potatoes while they are still warm allows the flavours to lift and develop. This great salad is evidence that simple, good ingredients don't need much done to them.

Devilicious potatoes with fresh chilli & capers

- 1kg (2lb 4oz) waxy salad potatoes, scrubbed
- 3 tbsp finely chopped fresh red chillies
- 150ml (1/4 pint) olive oil
- 150g (5 1/2oz) salted capers, soaked in cold water for 10 minutes
- 100g (3 1/2oz) flat leaf parsley, chopped
- salt
- sea salt crystals, to serve

Serves 4–6 | Vegetarian

1   Put the whole potatoes into a large saucepan, cover with at least 6cm (2 1/2in) cold water and add a pinch of salt. Bring to the boil, then reduce the heat and simmer for 25–30 minutes.

2   Meanwhile, mix the chopped chillies into the olive oil. Drain the capers, then squeeze them dry.

3   Test a potato by sliding a knife into the flesh and tapping the potato gently on the side of the pan. If the knife softly slips through the potato, it is ready; if it sticks, cook for a few more minutes. Once they are ready, drain the potatoes and set them on a plate to cool. While they are still warm, peel off the skins – they should come off easily. Break up the potatoes by hand and place on a serving dish. Sprinkle the capers and parsley over the top. Finish the dish by scattering over the wonderfully spicy chopped red chilli and drizzling over the oil. Scatter with a sprinkle of sea salt crystals.

Once you've mastered gnocchi with pesto, try different sauces. Stinging nettles have such a unique flavour – very subtle, but fresh. If you can't find any, use spinach, but you will miss out on the nettles' silky oils. Pick them with good-quality rubber gloves.

Savonese-style gnocchi with pesto

- 2kg (4lb 8oz) old potatoes
- 5 free-range eggs
- 3 tbsp olive oil
- 200g (7oz) '00' pasta flour, plus extra for dusting
- salt and pepper
- 1 quantity Basil pesto, to serve (*see* page 297)

Serves 4–6 | Vegetarian

1   Rinse the potatoes and put them whole into a large saucepan. Cover well with cold water and lightly season with salt. Bring to the boil, then reduce the heat and simmer for 35 minutes, or until a knife goes through the potatoes without any resistance but they are still slightly firm. Drain in a colander and allow to dry off.

2   Pass the potatoes through a potato ricer or a mouli on to a large wooden board. While still warm, make a well in the centre of the pile and break in the eggs. Add in the olive oil and season with salt and pepper. Dust the flour over the top of the pile and slowly pull the mixture together with your hands, trying not to crush the delicate structure of the potatoes – the lightest gnocchi requires the lightest of touches. Once you have a workable dough, give it a few good kneads together and then start to make the gnocchi.

3   Using a spatula, cut off a quarter of the dough and roll it into a rope about 2cm (3/4in) thick, then cut into 1.5cm (5/8in) lengths. Pick up each piece of gnocchi in turn and, using your thumb, press it on the fork tines. This creates the little grooves that your sauce will stick to. Reserve the prepared gnocchi on a tray dusted with flour and continue to make gnocchi until you have used up all the dough. Cover with a clean tea towel.

4   Bring a large saucepan of water to the boil, season it well with salt and drop your gnocchi into it in batches – they will sink to the bottom but not for long. When they rise to the top, after about 2 minutes, they are cooked. Scoop them out with a slotted spoon and tip them into a large bowl. Spoon half the pesto over the gnocchi and serve the remaining pesto separately.

Gnocchi with stinging nettles

- 1 quantity gnocchi (*see* above)
- 500g (1lb 2oz) small stinging nettle leaves
- 150g (5¹/₂oz) butter, melted
- 150g (5¹/₂oz) Parmesan cheese, finely grated
- salt and pepper

Serves 4–6 | Vegetarian

1   Make the gnocchi as described above. While they are cooking, cook the nettle leaves in a separate saucepan of salted boiling water for 2 minutes. Drain well in a colander and press out any remaining water with a potato masher. Transfer to a large bowl containing the melted butter. Add the Parmesan, season with salt and pepper and toss to mix. Pour the nettle sauce on top of the drained gnocchi and serve immediately.

Salads like this are a wonder –
simple to make, fresh to eat and
good for you. Little touches like
Japanese vinegar and fresh mint
lift the flavours even further. I use
a lovely salad potato, the Linska,
which is waxy enough but crumbles
perfectly. The cucumber must be
very fresh. Keep the skin on: it is full
of vitamins.

Potato &
cucumber salad

- 1kg (2lb 4oz) Linska or other salad
  potatoes, scrubbed
- 1 cucumber
- 4 tbsp Japanese vinegar
- 4 tbsp virgin olive oil
- 2 mint sprigs, chopped
- 4 tbsp sunflower seeds, lightly toasted
- salt and pepper

Serves 4–6 | Vegetarian

1   Put the whole potatoes into a large saucepan and cover with cold
water by a depth of at least 6cm (2¹/2in). Season the water with salt,
bring to the boil, then reduce the heat and simmer for 25–30 minutes.

2   Meanwhile, top and tail the cucumber, then cut it in half along its
length. Remove the seeds with a teaspoon, then chop it into 5cm (2in)
chunks and put them into a bowl. Sprinkle half the vinegar and olive
oil on to the cucumber and season with salt and pepper. Mix well with
your hands. Sprinkle with half the mint, then mix again and taste. Be
careful not to eat all the cucumber before the potatoes are cooked!

3   Test a potato by sliding a knife into the flesh, picking up the potato
with the knife and tapping it gently on the side of the pan. If the knife
softly slips through the potato, it is ready; if it sticks, cook for a few
more minutes. Once they are ready, drain the potatoes and set them
on a plate to cool. While they are still warm, peel off the skins – they
should come off easily. Break up the potatoes by hand on to a serving
dish and mix in the cucumber. Drizzle with the remaining vinegar and
oil, sprinkle with the rest of the mint and add a touch more salt and
pepper. Scatter the sunflower seeds on top and serve.

This salad is a festival of colour: sweet potatoes combined with oranges, plus parsley and pepper adding depth. It's another great salad to take out to a picnic.

Sweet potato salad with quinoa, orange & parsley

- 1kg (2lb 4oz) sweet potatoes
- olive oil, for drizzling
- 500g (1lb 2oz) quinoa
- 3 oranges
- 250g (9oz) flat leaf parsley, chopped
- 250ml (9fl oz) olive oil
- salt and pepper

Serves 4–6 | Vegetarian

1   Preheat the oven to 180°C/fan 160°C/gas mark 4. Peel the sweet potatoes and then cut them into 2cm (3/4in) cubes. Spread out on a roasting tray, drizzle lightly with olive oil and season with a little salt and pepper. Roast for 30 minutes, or until tender.

2   While the sweet potatoes are roasting, rinse the quinoa and put it into a saucepan. Pour over enough cold water to cover by a depth of about 3cm (1¼in) and bring to the boil. Reduce the heat, cover with a lid, leaving just a crack for the steam to escape, and cook for 16 minutes. Turn off the heat and leave to cool. Meanwhile, using a knife, peel the oranges and remove any white pith. Working over a large mixing bowl to catch the juice, cut the segments of flesh from between the membranes and add to the juice.

3   When the sweet potatoes are cooked, leave them to cool on the roasting tray, then transfer to the bowl with the oranges. Add the cooled quinoa and the parsley, drizzle in the olive oil and mix together lightly before serving in bowls.

I created this recipe because I thought it would be fun, but it's very tasty too. Creative, fun and delicious: well, that's just how I like my food to be. You could fill these pancakes with just about anything. Try halloumi cheese and tomatoes, the Celeriac remoulade on page 76 or my Preserved girolles on page 252.

Sweet potato pancakes with chilli & lime

- 100g (3¹/₂oz) plain flour
- 1 tbsp olive oil, plus 75ml (2¹/₂fl oz)
- 3 free-range egg yolks
- 300ml (¹/₂ pint) milk
- 50g (1³/₄oz) butter

Filling
- 1kg (2lb 4oz) sweet potatoes, cut into 2cm (³/₄in) cubes
- 1 cinnamon stick
- 1 garlic clove, chopped
- 1 tsp cumin seeds
- 1 tsp dried red chilli flakes
- juice of 3 limes
- 2 tbsp chopped mint
- salt and pepper
- 50g (1³/₄oz) Cheddar cheese, grated
- soured cream, to serve
- chervil sprigs, to garnish

Serves 4–6 | Vegetarian

1 To make the pancakes, put the flour into a mixing bowl and make a well in the centre. Add the tablespoon of olive oil and egg yolks to the well and, using a stiff balloon whisk, break up the eggs and blend in the flour until you have a thick, smooth paste. Start whisking in the milk, a third at a time. The consistency should be like smooth pouring cream.

2 Heat a large frying pan, add the butter and allow it to melt, then tip into a small bowl. Just before the residue of butter that is left in the pan begins to smoke, add enough batter to cover the base of the pan. Wait for the bubbles to appear through the pancake and then, using a spatula, flip the pancake over to colour the other side. When golden on each side, tip the pancake on to a cool, clean, dry surface – this cools the pancake quickly and prevents it from sweating. Repeat the process until all the batter is used up. Reserve the pancakes on a plate.

3 Put the sweet potato cubes into a saucepan, cover well with cold water and season with salt. Add the cinnamon stick and garlic to the pan and bring to the boil. Reduce the heat and simmer for 14 minutes, until tender. Meanwhile, heat a small frying pan over a medium-high heat, tip in the cumin seeds and shake the pan until they start to toast. Transfer to a mortar with the chilli flakes and crush.

4 Preheat the oven to 180°C/fan 160°C/gas mark 4. When the sweet potato is cooked, drain and place in a mixing bowl. Add the spice mix, lime juice, mint and the remaining 75ml (2¹/₂fl oz) olive oil. Mix gently, to keep the sweet potato intact. Season with pepper and check the salt. Lay a pancake on a work surface, spoon some sweet potato mixture in a line, slightly off-centre, then roll it up and place on a baking sheet. Continue with the remaining pancakes. Sprinkle with cheese and heat in the oven for 6 minutes. Serve with soured cream and some chervil.

The fish sauce in this soup really helps lift the flavours. This is the kind of soup I eat after training – it's good for you, clean-tasting and hearty.

Sweet potato & rice noodle soup with sesame oil & tofu

- 600g Thai dried rice noodles
- 500ml (18fl oz) Chicken stock (*see* page 296)
- 500ml (18fl oz) Vegetable stock (*see* page 297)
- 200g (7oz) sweet potato, cut into 3cm (1¼in) cubes and cooked until just tender
- 200g (7oz) firm tofu, cut into 3cm (1¼in) cubes
- 1 tsp Thai fish sauce
- 3 tbsp sesame oil
- 3 spring onions, finely sliced
- pepper

Serves 6

1   Prepare the rice noodles according to the packet instructions until just tender. Drain and set aside.

2   Put both stocks into another saucepan and bring to the boil. Add the sweet potato and tofu and boil for 1–2 minutes. Add the fish sauce and some freshly ground pepper, then turn off the heat.

3   Divide the rice noodles between serving bowls. Add the broth, sesame oil and spring onion, then serve immediately.

Fritti misti are deep-fried battered vegetables – use any that you like. Those suggested below are some of my favourites, but I love deep-fried mushrooms and pumpkin too. Build up your confidence by frying small batches and getting a feel for the oil and how the temperature drops when you add the veg.

Fritti misti

- **juice of 1 lemon**
- **6 large salsify**
- **6 courgette flowers, male and female, outsides cleaned with a soft brush**
- **200g (7oz) plain flour**
- **2 tbsp salt**
- **1 tbsp crushed black peppercorns**
- **2 sweet potatoes, scrubbed and cut into discs 1cm (½in) thick**
- **4 celery sticks**
- **12 sage leaves**
- **3 litres (5¼ pints) sunflower oil, for deep-frying**
- **1 quantity Tempura batter (*see* page 297)**
- **lemon cheeks, to serve (*see* step 4, page 44),**

Serves 4–6 | Vegetarian

1   Add the lemon juice to a bowl of cold water. Peel the salsify and put them into the bowl. Open the courgette flowers by running your finger to the heart of them, then gently push out and discard the stamen.

2   Mix the flour with the salt and crushed peppercorns. Remove a handful of salsify from the water, cut into bite-sized pieces and shake dry in a colander. Put the pieces into a clean, dry plastic bag and add 3 tablespoons of the seasoned flour. Hold the top of the bag closed and shake vigorously so the salsify is well coated. This helps the batter to stick to them. Tip into a sieve and shake off the excess flour. Repeat with the remaining salsify, the sweet potatoes, celery, sage leaves and courgette flowers.

3   Heat the sunflower oil in a deep, heavy-based saucepan to 180°C or until a cube of bread browns in 30 seconds. When the oil is ready, dip the floured vegetables into the batter and allow any excess to drip off. Add the battered pieces to the hot oil in batches and fry for about 3 minutes, until a pale golden colour. Remove with a slotted spoon and drain on kitchen paper. Keep warm while cooking the remaining batches. Sprinkle with sea salt and serve the fritti with lemon cheeks.

I know this combination sounds wacky to anyone not Stateside, but it actually tastes pretty good. This is my own twist on a traditional dish served at Thanksgiving with roast turkey and the trimmings. Maple syrup works really well with the rosemary.

Roasted sweet potato with marshmallows & maple syrup

– 2kg (4lb 8oz) sweet potatoes, scrubbed
– a handful of rosemary sprigs
– 100ml (3¹/₂fl oz) light olive oil
– 500g (1lb 2oz) marshmallows
– 250ml (9fl oz) maple syrup
– salt

Serves 4–6

1   Preheat the oven to 180°C/fan 160°C/gas mark 4 and line a roasting tray with baking parchment. Cut the sweet potatoes into chunks about 5–7cm (2–2³/₄in) thick, arrange in the prepared tray with the rosemary sprigs, then drizzle with the olive oil and sprinkle with a little salt. Roast in the oven for 25 minutes.

2   Remove the roasting tray from the oven and scatter the marshmallows on top. Drizzle maple syrup all over the tray, then return it to the oven and roast for a further 10 minutes. Serve warm.

I love walking through the markets of East London, which have the most amazing array of flavours from all over the world. Fufu is as much a staple in West Africa as mashed potato is in Britain, and this plantain stew goes perfectly with the fufu mash. Try adding sweet potato to the fufu and even a little fresh ginger.

Buttered yam fufu with plantain stew

- 2kg (4lb 8oz) yams
- 300ml (1/2 pint) milk
- 200g (7oz) butter,
  plus extra to serve
- whole nutmeg, for grating
- salt and pepper

Plantain stew
- 1 white onion, chopped
- 500ml (18fl oz) coconut milk
- 2 fresh red chillies, thinly sliced
- 50ml (2fl oz) lime juice
- 2 tbsp white wine vinegar
- 4 plantains
- 3 tbsp light olive oil
- 1 bunch coriander, finely chopped
- 6cm (2½in) piece of fresh root ginger,
  finely chopped
- salt and pepper

Serves 4–6 | Vegetarian

1   Cut the yams into large chunks about 6–7cm (2½–2¾in). Rinse thoroughly and put them into a large saucepan, cover well with cold water and add 2 good pinches of salt. Bring to the boil, then reduce the heat, skim off any white foam that rises to the surface and simmer for 35–40 minutes, or until a knife goes through the yams without any resistance but they are still slightly firm.

2   While the yams are simmering, prepare the plantain stew. Put the onion, 125ml (4fl oz) of the coconut milk, the chillies, lime juice and vinegar into a saucepan, season with salt and pepper and bring up to a simmer. Continue simmering over a medium heat for 15 minutes, or until the onion is soft.

3   Cut the plantains into 5–6cm (2–2½in) pieces. Heat the olive oil in a large frying pan and fry the plantain in batches over a medium-high heat for about 5 minutes on each side, until golden brown. Transfer the browned plantain to the coconut milk pan. Add the coriander and ginger and return to a medium heat, adding the rest of the coconut milk. Simmer for 5–7 minutes and check the seasoning.

4   While the plantain is simmering, drain the yams in a colander and allow to dry. Meanwhile, put the milk and butter into the empty saucepan over a low heat until the butter has melted. Remove from the heat, season lightly with salt and pepper and grate in a couple of strokes of nutmeg.

5   Pass the yams through a mouli or potato ricer set directly over the milk mixture and stir. Alternatively, drop the yams into the milk mixture and mash by hand with a potato masher. Check the seasoning and serve hot, topped with a knob of butter, alongside the plantain stew.

Skill: Roast

The recipes I've included here show the different results that can be achieved through roasting. I always use a fairly hot oven to roast my veggies; it creates a depth of flavour, caramelizing and crisping up the exposed edges and intensifying the flavours of the whole dish. I like to use the heat of the oven to cook a number of things at the same time, so try out a couple of these recipes together.

Roasted carrots with caraway & chilli cream

- 3 bunches of carrots (use different-coloured varieties if available)
- 2 garlic cloves, finely chopped
- 2 tsp caraway seeds
- 2 tsp dried red chilli flakes
- 75ml (2½fl oz) olive oil, plus an extra 1tsp
- 150ml (¼ pint) crème fraîche
- salt and pepper

Serves 6 | Vegetarian

1   Preheat the oven to 180°C/fan 160°C/gas mark 4 and line a roasting tray with baking parchment. Scrub the carrots and top and tail them. Roughly chop the bigger carrots, leaving the smaller ones whole. Put them all into a large mixing bowl and add the garlic, caraway seeds, half the chilli flakes and the 75ml (2½fl oz) olive oil. Season with salt and pepper and mix well.

2   Spread the carrot mixture out on the prepared tray and roast the carrots for 30 minutes, or until they are tender and turn a golden brown colour.

3   While the carrots are roasting, grind the rest of the chilli flakes in a pestle and mortar. Mix into the crème fraîche along with a hint of salt and pepper and the remaining teaspoon of olive oil.

4   When the carrots are cooked, remove them from the oven and arrange them on a serving plate. Spoon over the seasoned chilli cream – the heat will make it run all over the carrots, leaving a creamy residue on them and a lovely sauce to mop up.

My lovely roast veg

- 1 pale aubergine, topped and tailed
- 1 red onion, unpeeled
- 1 fennel bulb, trimmed
- 3 Jerusalem artichokes, scrubbed
- 1 small celeriac, scrubbed
- 4 oregano sprigs, leaves picked
- 1 fresh red chilli
- 1 garlic clove, chopped
- 75ml (2½fl oz) extra virgin olive oil
- 4 tbsp sesame seeds, lightly toasted
- salt and pepper
- bottle of balsamic vinegar, to serve

Serves 4–6 | Vegetarian

1   Preheat the oven to 180°C/fan 160°C/gas mark 4 and line a roasting tray with baking parchment. Cut the aubergine into different-shaped chunks all about 5–7cm (2–2¾in) in size. Cut the onion into 8 half-moons. Cut the fennel into 6 pieces through the core. Cut the Jerusalem artichokes in half lengthways. Trim the celeriac and then scrub it, keeping most of the outer skin on. Cut the celeriac into fairly small pieces, 2–3cm (¾–1¼in), since it will take the longest to cook. Put all the vegetables into a large mixing bowl. Add the oregano, the whole chilli, garlic and olive oil, season with salt and pepper and mix well.

2   Follow step 2 of the method on page 66, but roast for 45 minutes. Remove from the oven and sprinkle with the sesame seeds. Arrange all the vegetables on a large serving dish if you like, but better still, just bring the roasting tray to the table and serve straight from the pan. Offer the balsamic vinegar separately for sprinkling.

Roasted Jerusalem artichokes with sunflower seeds

- 700g (1lb 9oz) Jerusalem artichokes, topped and tailed
- 100g (3½oz) sunflower seeds
- 2 garlic cloves, finely chopped
- 1 tsp celery salt
- 1 tsp dried red chilli flakes
- 75ml (2½fl oz) olive oil
- juice and finely grated zest of 1 unwaxed lemon

Serves 4–6 | Vegetarian

1   Preheat the oven to 180°C/fan 160°C/gas mark 4 and line a roasting tray with baking parchment. Scrub the artichokes – the skin develops a lovely flavour from roasting. Cut them in half lengthways and put them into a mixing bowl. Sprinkle in the sunflower seeds, garlic, celery salt, chilli flakes, olive oil and lemon zest and mix well.

2   Follow step 2 of the method on page 66. I like my Jerusalem artichokes still a little bit firm to the bite, but if you want them softer, roast them for a little longer, but be careful not to burn the sunflower seeds. Remove from the oven, squeeze over the lemon juice and serve. Any leftovers are great in salads.

Roasted parsnips & turnips with pork chops

- 600g (1lb 5oz) baby parsnips, topped and tailed
- 600g (1lb 5oz) baby turnips, topped and tailed
- 6 garlic cloves
- 2 tsp fennel seeds
- 100ml (3½fl oz) olive oil
- 6 pork chops, about 175–200g (6–7oz) each
- 50g (1¾oz) butter
- 3 tbsp Apple jam (*see* page 298)
- salt and pepper

Serves 6

1   Preheat the oven to 180°C/fan 160°C/gas mark 4 and line a roasting tray with baking parchment. Scrub the parsnips and turnips and put them into a large mixing bowl. Add the garlic cloves, half the fennel seeds and all the olive oil and season.

2   Follow step 2 of the method on page 66, roasting for 25 minutes. Meanwhile, lay the pork chops in a cold frying pan and place over a high heat to render some of the fat before the heat starts to colour the meat. Fry the chops for 8 minutes on each side until cooked, adding the butter to the pan when turning over. Crush the remaining fennel seeds into 1 teaspoon salt in a mortar and sprinkle over the chops. Serve with the roots and a dollop of your homemade Apple jam.

Roasted celeriac with celery salt & crispy bacon

- 750g (1lb 10oz) celeriac, scrubbed
- 2 tbsp chopped flat leaf parsley
- 2 tbsp wholegrain mustard
- 1 garlic clove, chopped
- 1 tsp celery salt
- 12 streaky bacon rashers
- pepper

Serves 4–6

1   Preheat the oven to 180°C/fan 160°C/gas mark 4 and line a roasting tray with baking parchment. Cut the celeriac into quarters, then cut the quarters into different-shaped chunks all about 3–4cm (1¼–1½in) in size. Put the celeriac pieces into a bowl and add the parsley, mustard and garlic. Mix well and season with the celery salt and pepper.

2   Follow step 2 of the method on page 66. Remove the tray from the oven. Lay the bacon rashers over the celeriac and return to the oven for 10 minutes, or until the bacon is lightly crispy. Serve hot.

Roasted butternut squash with chilli & soured cream

- 1 large butternut squash, topped and tailed
- 1 tsp dried red chilli flakes
- 3 garlic cloves, chopped
- 200ml (7fl oz) olive oil, plus extra for the chilli
- 200ml (7fl oz) soured cream
- 3 tbsp finely chopped fresh red chilli
- salt and pepper

Serves 4–6 | Vegetarian

1   Preheat the oven to 180°C/fan 160°C/gas mark 4 and line a roasting tray with baking parchment. Top and tail the squash and then cut it sideways through the middle. Using a serrated knife, trim off the skin, and cut the bottom piece in half and scoop out and discard the seeds. Cut all the flesh into fairly large chunks, about 5cm (2in). Put the squash pieces into a large mixing bowl, add the chilli flakes and garlic and season well. Drizzle in the olive oil and mix. Put the chopped red chilli in a small bowl and cover with olive oil, then set aside.

2   Follow step 2 of the method on page 66, then check to see if the squash is tender – some squashes cook a little quicker than others, depending on the season and how much water they contain. Return to the oven and roast for a few minutes more if necessary. When cooked, transfer to a serving plate. Dollop and drizzle over the soured cream and then spoon over the fresh chilli in olive oil.

Roasted courgettes with pumpkin seeds

- 400g (14oz) yellow courgettes, topped and tailed
- 400g (14oz) green courgettes, topped and tailed
- 3 shallots, roughly diced
- 3 tbsp pumpkin seeds
- 150ml (¼ pint) olive oil
- salt and pepper

Serves 4–6 | Vegetarian

1   Preheat the oven to 190°C/fan 170°C/gas mark 5 and line a roasting tray with baking parchment. Cut the courgettes into different-shaped pieces about 6 x 2.5cm (2½ x 1in) in size. Put them into a bowl. Add the shallots to the bowl with the pumpkin seeds and season with salt and pepper. Drizzle in the olive oil and mix well.

2   Follow step 2 of the method on page 66, but roast for 20 minutes. Serve hot.

This is such a pretty dish, and what I like about it is that under the gorgeous façade is a peppery, punchy, fresh little salad full of flavour, colours and hidden gems. You absolutely must serve this salad at a summer party, sitting outside while watching the sun set.

Radish salad with pomegranate & cannellini beans

- 1 bunch of radishes
- 1 pomegranate
- 1 bunch of wild rocket
- few leaves oak leaf lettuce
- 500 g (1lb 2oz) cooked cannellini beans
- juice of 1 lemon
- 75ml (2¹/2fl oz) olive oil
- salt and pepper

Serves 4–6 | Vegetarian

1   Top and tail the radishes, then drop them into iced water while you prepare the rest of the salad – this not only cleans them, but firms them up to a nice crunch.

2   Crack open the pomegranate, pick out the ruby red seeds and put them into a bowl – be gentle and try not to bruise or break them, as you want them to pop in your mouth when you eat this salad.

3   Put the rocket and lettuce into a salad bowl. Drain the radishes and cut into all different shapes and sizes, even keeping some of them whole, and drop them into the salad bowl, along with half the pomegranate seeds. Squeeze in the lemon juice, season with salt and pepper and drizzle in the olive oil. Mix lightly and serve on individual plates with the rest of the pomegranate seeds sprinkled over the top.

By the time autumn and the root vegetable season roll around, your body is craving hearty dishes – bowls of steaming goodness to see you through the dark nights. Then the miracle of spring makes you forget all about these wonderful dishes until winter sets in again.

Swede casserole with parsley, white wine & lamb neck

– 750g (1lb 10oz) swede
– 500g (1lb 2oz) potatoes
– 1 bunch of flat leaf parsley
– 500ml (18fl oz) medium-dry white wine
– 1 litre (1³/4 pints) Vegetable stock (*see* page 297)
– 750g (1lb 10oz) lamb neck, trimmed of fat and gristle
– salt and pepper
– chervil sprigs, to garnish

Serves 4–6

1   Cut the swede and potatoes into equal-sized chunks, about 3cm (1¹/4in). Put them into a large flameproof casserole dish. Pick the parsley leaves from their stalks and chop the stalks, then add to the pan. Add the wine, stock, lamb and seasoning, then bring to the boil, skimming off any white foam that rises to the surface.

2   Reduce the heat to a light simmer. Place the lid on top and cook for about 1¹/2 hours, or until the meat and vegetables are tender, checking from time to time that the liquid hasn't boiled away. Chop most of the parsley leaves and add to the dish just before serving. Add a sprig of chervil to each plate.

Putting together some of the most basic vegetables might not sound extraordinary, but I challenge you not to remember this recipe once you have cooked it. It feels like it's doing you good as you eat it, and it gets better a day or two later. You can be generous with the ingredients too – spice it up a little, or rev up the garlic and ginger if you're feeling cold. Make double quantities and enjoy it reheated the next day.

Root vegetable broth with fresh ginger & soy sauce

- 100ml (3½fl oz) olive oil
- 250g (9oz) white onion, cut into 3cm (1¼in) cubes
- 250g (9oz) celery, cut into 3cm (1¾in) pieces
- 1 garlic clove, cut in half
- 2 bay leaves
- 50g (1¾oz) flat leaf parsley, leaves picked and stalks finely chopped
- 6cm x 2.5cm (2½in x 1in) piece of fresh root ginger, chopped into slivers
- 250g (9oz) swede, cut into 3cm (1¼in) cubes
- 250g (9oz) turnip, cut into 3cm (1¼in) cubes
- 250g (9oz) carrot, cut into 3cm (1¼in) cubes
- 250g (9oz) potato, cut into 3cm (1¼in) cubes
- 250g (9oz) parsnip, cut into 3cm (1¼in) cubes
- 1.5 litres (2¾ pints) Vegetable stock (*see* page 297)
- 50ml (2fl oz) light soy sauce, or to taste
- salt and pepper

Serves 4–6 | Vegetarian

1   Heat the olive oil in a large, heavy-based saucepan, add the onion and celery and cook over a medium heat for 5 minutes, stirring occasionally. Add the garlic and bay leaves and cook for another 5 minutes, then add the chopped parsley stalks and the ginger. Add all the root vegetables and stir well. Continue to stir and cook the vegetables for 5 minutes as the heat builds in the pan and starts the flavours flowing. Season with salt and pepper, being careful with the salt, as soy sauce will be added later.

2   Pour in the stock and bring to the boil, skimming off any white foam that rises to the surface. Now reduce the heat, put the lid half on to prevent too much evaporation and simmer for 40 minutes. Chop the parsley leaves roughly and add to the broth, drizzle in the amount of soy sauce to your liking and check the pepper – you might need some more.

Remoulade is a classic salad that's absolutely lovely. Serve it with a ploughman's lunch or a piece of fish, or as a light snack with toast and cornichons. It's also great in a sandwich with a slice of ham.

Celeriac remoulade

- 50g (1¾oz) salted capers, soaked in cold water for 10 minutes
- 25g (1oz) fresh horseradish root
- 3 tbsp Homemade mayonnaise (*see* page 297)
- 500g (1lb 2oz) celeriac
- 2 tbsp finely chopped flat leaf parsley
- salt and pepper

Serves 4–6 | Vegetarian

1   Drain and chop the capers. Peel the horseradish and grate finely. Put the mayonnaise in a bowl and add both the capers and horseradish.

2   Cut the celeriac in half, then stand each half on its flat side and slice as thinly as possible. Pile the slices on top of each other in stacks of 10, then cut the stacks into thin matchsticks.

3   Add the celeriac matchsticks and chopped parsley to the mayonnaise mixture, season lightly and mix together.

Swede remoulade with mustard & celery salt

- 500g (1lb 2oz) swede
- 1 tbsp wholegrain mustard
- juice of 1 lemon
- 4 tbsp Homemade mayonnaise (*see* page 297)
- 1 tsp celery salt
- pepper

Serves 4–6 | Vegetarian

1   Cut the swede in half, then stand each half on its flat side and slice as thinly as possible. Pile the slices on top of each other in stacks of 10, then cut the stacks into thin matchsticks.

2   Put the swede matchsticks into a bowl and add the mustard, lemon juice and mayonnaise. Season with the celery salt and a little pepper, then mix well.

I have used celeriac in so many different ways – poaching, roasting, frying, mashing, grilling and even raw. It's super-versatile, tastes fantastic and should be on everyone's shopping list when it's in season.

Celeriac tower with spring leaves

- 750g (1lb 10oz) celeriac
- 1 head of oak leaf lettuce
- 1 head of frisée lettuce
- 1 bunch of spring onions
- 1 bunch of radishes
- 2 tbsp chopped chervil
- 150ml (1/4 pint) Shallot dressing (*see* page 297)
- salt

Serves 4–6 | Vegetarian

1   Cut the celeriac into discs 1cm (1/2in) thick. Drop them into a saucepan of salted boiling water and cook for 2 minutes. Drain and leave to cool.

2   Tear the lettuce leaves into pieces and place in a large mixing bowl. Trim the spring onions and radishes and slice into discs 2cm (3/4in) thick. Add them to the bowl along with the chopped chervil, then drizzle in the dressing. Mix the salad lightly with your fingertips.

3   To build a tower, arrange 1 disc of celeriac on a plate and put some salad on top. Place another disc of celeriac on top of the salad, and put some more salad on top of that. Repeat this process, using at least 4 discs of celeriac, but you could be flash and go for more if you like. Finish the tower with a disc of celeriac, a piece of lettuce and a drizzle of the dressing.

Turnips make a brilliant addition to so many dishes. Buying them large gives you robust flavour, great for soups and mash. Using them young gives you sweet, delicate flavour. This recipe works well with any baby vegetables that are around in the summer months.

Braised & glazed baby turnips, carrots & fennel

- 500g (1lb 2oz) baby turnips, scrubbed
- 500g (1lb 2oz) baby carrots, scrubbed
- 500g (1lb 2oz) baby fennel
- 1 litre (1¾ pints) Vegetable stock (*see* page 297)
- 75g (2¾oz) butter
- 2 tsp caster sugar
- 2 bay leaves
- salt and pepper
- chervil sprigs, to garnish

Serves 4–6 | Vegetarian

1   Trim the leaves from the turnips and carrots, and trim the feathery tops from the fennel. Put all the vegetables into a saucepan large enough to hold them. Add the rest of the ingredients, season with salt and pepper and place over a medium-high heat. Cook for 16–18 minutes to allow the liquid to evaporate: in doing so, it will leave behind a buttery, sticky, flavourful glazing liquor.

2   Shake the pan, letting the vegetables roll around until lightly glazed. Turn off the heat, cover the pan and leave the veg to absorb the flavours for 4–6 minutes. Serve warm, garnished with parsley sprigs.

Baby leeks, squash & fennel

Take 500g (1lb 2oz) baby leeks, discard the outer leaves and cut off the dark green tops. Wash thoroughly. Trim the feathery tops from 500g (1lb 2oz) fennel and discard any tough outer leaves. Peel and chop 500g (1lb 2oz) baby squash. Follow the method as above.

I always laugh at the poor perception of turnips –
they have such a lowly image in many people's eyes,
but nothing could be further from the truth, as this
dish proves. Serve these hot with some steamed pak
choi, or enjoy them cold at a picnic. For vegetarians,
tofu can be substituted for the pork.

Baby turnips stuffed with chives, ginger & pork

- **12 small young turnips**
- **350g (12oz) pork fillet, chopped into very small pieces, like mince**
- **3 tbsp very finely chopped chives**
- **2 tbsp very finely chopped fresh root ginger**
- **3 tbsp light soy sauce**
- **1 tbsp Thai fish sauce**
- **pepper**

Serves 4–6

1   Peel the turnips and put them into a saucepan. Cover well with cold water and bring to the boil. Reduce the heat and simmer for 25 minutes, or until the turnips are soft but with a slight bite to them. Drain and refresh them in cold water. Using a small, sharp knife (or a melon baller or the tip of a peeler), cut out a divot 2cm ($3/4$in) round and 1cm ($1/2$in) deep from the top of each turnip. Reserve the turnips while you make the stuffing.

2   Put the pork into a bowl and mix in the chives and ginger, then add the soy sauce and fish sauce. Add some freshly ground pepper and mix well. Spoon the mixture into the cavities of the turnips, piling them up nice and high. Arrange the turnips in a bamboo steamer or on a trivet inside a saucepan and steam for 8–10 minutes, until the pork is cooked and the turnips are hot.

Baby turnips with tofu stuffing

Prepare and cook the turnips as in step 1 above. Replace the minced pork with 350g (12oz) plain fresh tofu, then stuff and steam the turnips as in step 2.

The colour of this vegetable is something special that is certainly worth preserving. Cooking salsify in flour water, as below, keeps it white.

Warmed salsify salad with smoked mackerel

- 4 tbsp plain flour
- 1kg (2lb 4oz) salsify
- 1 bunch of radishes
- 4 smoked mackerel fillets, skin removed
- 50ml (2fl oz) olive oil
- 1 head of frisée lettuce
- 100ml (3¹/₂fl oz) House dressing (*see* page 297)
- salt

Serves 4–6

1   Put the flour into a saucepan and mix in enough cold water to make a sticky paste, then slowly add more water until it has the consistency of milk. Bring the flour water to a soft rolling boil, then drop in the salsify and cook for 8–10 minutes, until just tender. Meanwhile top and tail the radishes and cut discs from the centre of each radish, discarding (or eating) the rest. Pour away the liquid from the salsify and leave it to cool to room temperature.

2   Break each mackerel fillet into 2 pieces. Warm a frying pan and add the olive oil. Slice the salsify into strips and fry gently for 3–4 minutes on each side, until golden brown, adding the mackerel to the pan halfway through.

3   Arrange the lettuce on a serving plate and sprinkle over the radish slices. Place the warm salsify and mackerel on top, season with salt and drizzle with the dressing.

Garlic
Shallot
Onion
Leek
Fennel
Kohlrabi
Celery
Asparagus
Samphire

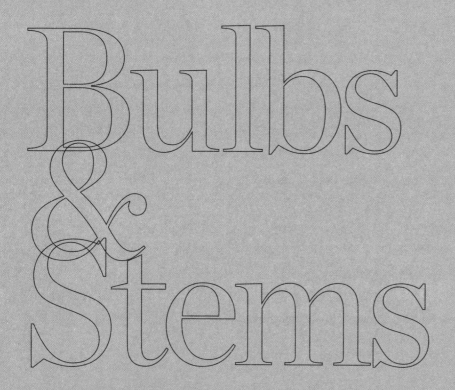

Bulbs
&
Stems

On a hot day this soup will rock anyone's taste buds. I learned to make it in Spain, where people eat it all the time. It's basically a white gazpacho and the large amount of garlic is mellowed by the bread: it is so refreshing,

White garlic soup with almonds

- 150g (5½oz) whole blanched almonds
- milk, for soaking
- 4 slices of white bread, crusts removed
- 4 garlic cloves
- 100ml (3½fl oz) olive oil
- 2 tbsp sherry vinegar
- 300ml (½ pint) cold water
- salt and pepper
- flaked almonds, to garnish

Serves 4–6 | Vegetarian

1 Soak the almonds in milk for at least 1 hour or overnight. Soak the bread in milk for 10 minutes.

2 Drain the soaked almonds and bread but don't squeeze the bread dry. Put them into a blender with the garlic cloves and blend to a smooth paste. With the motor still running, drizzle in the olive oil, then the vinegar and finally the water – blend until you reach a consistency somewhat similar to single cream.

3 Transfer the soup to a bowl and season with salt and pepper. Cover with clingfilm and chill in the refrigerator for at least 1 hour.

4 While the soup is chilling, heat a dry frying pan over a medium heat, tip in the flaked almonds and shake the pan until they start to toast, but watch carefully so that they don't burn. Serve the soup sprinkled with the toasted flaked almonds.

This dish begins with the aroma of garlic and rosemary frying in butter, and you get hungrier and hungrier while you cook it. You could use thyme or even basil instead, but rosemary is wicked when fried.

Penne with garlic, rosemary & mascarpone

- 400g (14oz) dried penne
- 50g (1¾oz) butter
- 2 garlic cloves, very thinly sliced
- 3 tbsp rosemary leaves
- 2 tbsp pine nuts
- 100g (3½oz) mascarpone cheese
- juice of 1 lemon
- 75g (2¾oz) Parmesan cheese, freshly grated
- salt and pepper

Serves 4–6 | Vegetarian

1   Cook the penne in a large saucepan of salted boiling water for 10–12 minutes, or according to the packet instructions, until al dente.

2   Meanwhile, melt the butter in another saucepan, add the garlic and rosemary and cook over a medium heat until the butter starts to bubble. Add in lots of pepper at this stage, and just before the garlic begins to turn brown add the pine nuts. Drain the cooked penne, reserving 2–3 tablespoons of the cooking water. Add the pasta and reserved water to the rosemary pan – the water stops the garlic from browning further.

3   Add the mascarpone, lemon juice and half the Parmesan. Stir well, check the seasoning and serve straight away, finishing the dish by sprinkling over the remaining Parmesan.

When you poach shallots they become really sweet, and with the succulent strips of chicken and the floating dumpling, this is definitely a complete meal in itself. The star anise adds an aromatic quality, and with a few sprigs of chervil this soup is complete.

Chicken soup with poached shallots & dumplings

- 1 medium free-range chicken, about 1.6kg (3lb 8 oz)
- 1 tbsp whole black peppercorns
- 3 bay leaves
- 2 juniper berries
- 2 star anise
- 1 white onion, cut into 3cm (1¼in) cubes
- 1 head of celery, trimmed and cut into 3cm (1¼in) cubes
- 1kg (2lb 4oz) carrots, scrubbed and cut into 3cm (1¼in) cubes
- 8 shallots, halved sideways through the middle
- olive oil, for drizzling
- chervil sprigs, to garnish

Dumplings
- 500g (1lb 2oz) self-raising flour
- 250g (9oz) vegetable suet
- about 100ml (3½fl oz) cold water

Serves 4–6

1   Put the chicken into a large saucepan, cover with cold water and bring to the boil. Skim off the white foam that rises to the surface, then reduce the heat to a simmer. Add the peppercorns, bay leaves, juniper berries and star anise and simmer for 20 minutes. Add the onion, celery and carrots and continue to simmer for another 40 minutes, or until the chicken is tender.

2   Lift the chicken out of the pan, transfer it to a large plate and leave until cool enough to handle. Peel off and discard the skin, then remove the meat from the bones, cut into chunks and set aside.

3   Skim the fat from the chicken broth, then strain it through a fairly fine sieve into a saucepan, discarding the spices and vegetables. Bring the broth to a simmer, drop in the shallot halves and continue simmering for 20 minutes, then check the seasoning – avoid seasoning before this point, as you will have been reducing the liquid and therefore increasing the saltiness.

4   Meanwhile, prepare the dumplings. Put the flour into a bowl, add the suet and parsley and stir in enough of the cold water to bring the mixture together, but avoid making it too wet. Form into 12 small balls in the palms of your hands.

5   Add the dumplings to the broth and simmer, uncovered, for 5 minutes, then add the chicken chunks and simmer for another 5 minutes, rolling the dumplings around occasionally. Ladle the soup into big bowls, drop in a few chervil sprigs and serve.

You can serve these shallots with roast aubergine, chicken – hey, anything you like, but sometimes I like to let them cool and eat them in place of pickled onions as part of a ploughman's lunch.

Caramelized shallots in butter & palm sugar

- 500g (1lb 2oz) small round shallots
- 50g (1¾oz) butter
- 500ml (18fl oz) Vegetable stock (*see* page 297)
- 3 bay leaves
- 100g (3½oz) palm or light brown sugar
- salt and pepper

Serves 4–6 | **Vegetarian**

1   Put the whole shallots into a saucepan large enough for them all to be touching the base, add the butter and cook over a medium heat until they begin to colour on the underside. Roll the shallots over with a wooden spoon and continue to cook, rolling occasionally, until they are lightly browned on all sides.

2   Pour in the stock, add the bay leaves and season with salt and pepper. While the liquid is bubbling away over a medium heat, add the sugar and mix it in well. Continue cooking for 14–15 minutes, until all the liquid has evaporated and you are left with a lovely, sticky, caramelly pan of shallots.

Once baked, the sweet flesh of
Spanish onions has no comparison.
Smooth, slippery and stunning
to look at, serve these onions at a
dinner party and the conversation
will soon flow around the wonderful
simplicity of food. Look out for
extra large leeks to make the
simple variations too.

Salt-baked Spanish onions & garlic

- **6 large white Spanish onions, unpeeled**
- **2kg (4lb 8oz) rock salt**
- **2 garlic bulbs**
- **1 quantity Sauce soubise to serve**
  (*see* **page 298),**

Serves 4–6 | Vegetarian

1   Preheat the oven to 180°C/fan 160°C/gas mark 4. Trim and
clean up the onions without removing their outer skins. Spread
the salt out on a roasting tray. Arrange the onions and garlic bulbs
base-down and an equal distance apart on top of the salt.

2   Roast the onions and garlic for 40 minutes. Take them out of
the oven and, while still hot, cut the tops off with a pair of kitchen
scissors. Serve on the tray, with some Sauce soubise on the side.
Tell your guests to squeeze each onion and garlic bulb from the base
so that the baked flesh pops out of the holes.

Salt-baked leeks

Preheat the oven as above and peel off the outermost layer from
3 leeks. Cut the leeks into 8cm (3 in) pieces. Stand the pieces up
on the salt, prepared as above, and drop a knob of butter on each
piece. Bake for 30 minutes, until the butter is caramelized and the
leeks are turning brown.

In Normandy this soup is made with cider, but in the rest of France they use white wine. I could have called it English onion soup, as I used Cheddar cheese and Somerset cider. The cider is really pungent when you start to add it, but it mellows with the cooking process. Ahhh, I can smell it now...

French onion soup with cheesy crostini

- **6 large white onions**
- **150g (5¹/₂oz) butter**
- **1 bouquet garni of ¹/₂ leek, thyme, parsley, sage sprigs and bay leaves, tied together with string**
- **1 litre (1³/₄ pints) sweet cider**
- **150g (5¹/₂oz) plain flour**
- **1 litre (1³/₄ pints) Vegetable stock (*see* page 297)**
- **salt and pepper**

Crostini
- **1 French bread stick**
- **60g (2¹/₄oz) Cheddar cheese**

Serves 4–6 | Vegetarian

1   Slice the onions as thinly as possible. Put them into a saucepan, add half the butter and cook over a low heat for 35–40 minutes, or until golden brown, stirring occasionally – the longer you colour the onions, the bigger the flavour. Add the bouquet garni and cider, bring to a simmer and continue simmering for 10 minutes.

2   Meanwhile, melt the rest of the butter in a saucepan until it foams. Mix in the flour and cook over a low heat, stirring, for 8–10 minutes, until the roux turns a light golden brown. Pour in the stock and bring to the boil, whisking constantly. Reduce the heat and simmer for 15–20 minutes.

3   Add the cooked onion mixture to the soup and cook for a further 10 minutes. Check the seasoning.

4   Preheat the grill to medium. Slice the French stick into thin rounds, a maximum of 2cm (³/₄in) thick. Grate the Cheddar on to the bread and grill until golden brown. Pour the soup into bowls, and place a cheesy crostini on top of each. Serve straight away.

This is a really pretty dish. Keep all the ingredients very fresh and your guests can dress the salad themselves at the last moment. Serve up a couple of large handfuls of alfalfa sprouts for them to sprinkle over the salad and it's a completely different experience!

Insalata mista

- 200g (7oz) asparagus spears
- 1 large white onion
- 1 carrot
- 4 Baby Gem lettuces
- 100g (3½oz) cooked beetroot
- 1 beef tomato
- 3 free-range eggs, hard-boiled
- 200g (7oz) green olives
- 200g (7oz) can high-
  quality tuna

To serve
- light olive oil
- white wine vinegar
- salt and pepper

Serves 4–6

1   Trim the woody bases off the asparagus and discard. Cook the asparagus in a large saucepan of lightly salted boiling water for 4 minutes. Drain, leave to cool, then cut in half lengthways.

2   Thinly slice the onion into rings. Cut the carrot in half and chop the two halves into matchsticks. Pull the lettuce apart and cut into bite-sized pieces. Thinly slice the beetroot and tomato into discs. Shell the eggs, then cut them into quarters.

3   Arrange all the salad ingredients on a large serving plate. Drain the tuna and place in the centre of the salad. Serve the condiments on the side – the idea is to drizzle over the olive oil first, followed by the vinegar and then season with salt and pepper.

Winter salad

When asparagus is out of season, trim 4 young leeks, wash them thoroughly and blanch in hot water for 5 minutes. Replace the tuna with 200g (7oz) sardines, and make it funky by replacing the white onion with a large red onion.

I love making pizzas and have tried so many styles but always come back to a super-thin crust with minimal toppings. These recipes make four large individual pizza-style tarts, but you can make them smaller if you want to. The onion topping takes a long time to make, but it's worth it, and pestoso is a mixture of tomato sauce and pesto. You can also experiment with other toppings: try adding black olives or some smoked ham.

Onion & anchovy pizza

- 2.5kg (5lb 8oz) white Spanish onions, sliced
- 4 garlic cloves, unpeeled
- 100ml (3½fl oz) olive oil
- 1 quantity Pizza dough (*see* page 296)
- 12 anchovy fillets
- 1 tsp oregano

Serves 4

1   Put the onions, garlic and oil into a heavy-based saucepan, set over a low heat and cook for 2 hours, stirring occasionally.

2   Preheat the oven to 180°C/fan 160°C/gas mark 4 and put a baking sheet or pizza stone into the oven to heat up. Divide the dough into 4 pieces and roll or use your hands to stretch a piece into a round about 25cm (10in) in diameter and 4mm (¼in) thick (it will try to spring back, but carry on until you win the battle). Leave the dough to rise again for 10 minutes, covered.

3   Discard the garlic cloves from the onions, which will be sticky and caramelized, and season lightly with salt and pepper. Spread the onions over the dough bases, making sure not to include too much oil from the pan. Arrange the anchovies on top and sprinkle over the oregano. Using a large spatula or two, lift the pizza on to the hot baking sheet or pizza stone and bake for 15 minutes. Make the remaining pizzas in the same way.

Rocket pizza with goats' cheese & pestoso

- 1 quantity Pizza dough (*see* page 296)
- 1 quantity Classic tomato sauce (*see* page 211)
- 1 quantity Basil pesto (*see* page 297)
- 200g (7oz) goats' cheese, cut into chunks
- 1 tbsp chopped basil
- olive oil, for drizzling
- 2 bunches of wild rocket
- 65g (2¼oz) Parmesan cheese, freshly grated
- salt and pepper

Serves 4 | Vegetarian

1   Preheat the oven and prepare the dough as in step 2 above.

2   Divide the dough into 4 pieces and roll a piece into a circle about 25cm (10in) in diameter. Use a spatula or two to lift it on to the hot baking sheet or pizza stone and bake for 10 minutes..

3   Remove the baking sheet or pizza stone from the oven. Dollop the tomato sauce on to the pizza base, add the pesto, then use the back of the spoon in a circular motion to spread out the sauce mixture so that it reaches almost the edge of the dough base. Arrange the goats' cheese on top and then the basil. Drizzle with olive oil and season. Return to the oven and bake for about 6 minutes, or to your liking. Sprinkle over the rocket and Parmesan before serving.

4   Repeat steps 2 and 3 to make 3 more pizzas.

Feast: Mediterranean

I have long savoured the Mediterranean's wonderful rich culinary history and all of its seasonal and regional differences, from coastal villages to mountain ranges. I have captured here some of the flavours from my experiences in Italy, Spain and France. This isn't an entirely vegetarian feast, but every dish shines thanks to the vegetable ingredients. Tiger prawns and borlotti beans is a Tuscan dish, the raw courgette salad is from Sicily, the ceviche of sardines is from Perpignan, and the tomato pestoso spaghetti is from Genoa. There's a Piedmontese bagna cauda with iced celery and a Spanish asparagus tortilla. To complete the feast, serve with prosciutto di Parma, olives and some breadsticks for a fresh and sunny Mediterranean spread.

Mediterranean

1 Borlotti beans with tiger prawns & green chillies

- 600g (1lb 5oz) borlotti beans, podded weight
- 1 handful of flat leaf parsley stalks
- 50ml (2fl oz) white wine vinegar
- 100ml (3½fl oz) olive oil
- 1 fresh green chilli, deseeded and cut into half-moons
- 18 raw tiger prawns, peeled, tails intact
- salt and pepper

Serves 4–6

1 Put the borlotti beans into a saucepan with the parsley stalks, vinegar, half the olive oil and a few of the chilli pieces. Cover with cold water to a depth of about 7cm (2¾in) and bring to the boil. Reduce the heat and simmer for about an hour, until tender. Season and turn off the heat.

2 Cover the base of a frying pan with a thin film of water, add the remaining olive oil and place over a medium heat. When hot, add the prawns and cook for a maximum of 3 minutes, gently rolling them as and when they need it, until nearly cooked. Add the remaining chilli pieces and the warm beans. Turn off the heat and let the flavours combine for a minute before serving.

2 Raw courgette salad

- 5 courgettes, thinly sliced into ovals
- 2 tbsp finely chopped mint
- 1 tbsp deseeded and finely chopped fresh red chilli
- 75ml (2½fl oz) olive oil
- juice of 1 lemon
- salt and pepper

Serves 4–6 | Vegetarian

1 Put the courgette slices into a large colander and sprinkle lightly with salt. Set the colander over a bowl and leave for 20 minutes so the liquid from the courgettes drains into the bowl. Lightly spray the courgettes with water, then pat dry.

2 Put the courgettes into a mixing bowl and add three-quarters of the mint and chilli and all the olive oil and lemon juice. Season lightly with salt and pepper and mix well with your fingertips. Arrange on a serving plate and scatter with the remaining mint and chilli.

3 Iced celery bagna cauda

- 8 garlic cloves
- 15 salted anchovies, rinsed well
- 250ml (9fl oz) milk, plus extra for loosening
- 200g (7oz) butter, cut into small pieces
- 200ml (7fl oz) extra virgin olive oil
- 1 head of celery, separated into stalks
- pepper

Serves 4–6 | Vegetarian

1 Put the garlic cloves and anchovies into a small saucepan, cover with the milk and cook slowly over a low heat for 25–35 minutes, until the garlic is completely soft and the anchovies have broken up. Meanwhile, melt the butter in a separate saucepan. Transfer the hot milky garlic and anchovies to a blender and blend to a smooth paste. With the motor still running, drizzle in the warm melted butter, then drizzle in the olive oil, a quarter at a time, taking care that the mixture doesn't become too thick, otherwise it will split. To loosen the mixture if necessary, add a little milk. When the oil is all incorporated, taste and add pepper. Keep the mixture warm in a bowl over a saucepan of hot water until ready to serve – it will be good for at least an hour.

2 Place the celery stalks in a bowl of iced water for 15 minutes. Serve with the sauce.

4 Fennel & sardine ceviche

- 1 large fennel bulb, fronds removed and very thinly sliced
- 1 large carrot, very thinly sliced
- 1 tsp black peppercorns
- 6 fresh sardines, filleted and the small bones removed (12 fillets required)
- juice of 2 lemons
- 2 tbsp herb vinegar
- 250ml (9fl oz) light olive oil
- sea salt

Serves 4–6

1 Arrange half the fennel and carrot slices in the bottom of a baking dish, then season with sea salt and some whole black peppercorns. Arrange the sardine fillets, skin-side up, then cover with the remaining fennel and carrot.

2 Squeeze the lemon juice over the whole dish and sprinkle with the vinegar. Pour over the olive oil and shake the dish so that all the fish is sitting in the liquid. Season with salt and the remaining peppercorns, then chop the reserved fennel fronds and sprinkle over the fish. Set aside for 30 minutes so that the fish is fairly well cooked in the acidic mixture and the fennel will have released some of its lovely sweet, pungent oils. Marinate for an hour for it to be cooked through. Transfer to a platter to serve.

5 Spaghetti with raw tomato pestoso

- 750g (1lb 10oz) tomatoes, cut into bite-sized pieces
- 1 garlic clove, very finely chopped
- 2 tbsp herb vinegar
- 4 tbsp olive oil, plus extra for drizzling
- 750g (1lb 10oz) dried spaghetti
- 4 tbsp Basil pesto (see page 297)
- salt and pepper

Serves 4–6 | Vegetarian

1 Put the tomatoes and garlic in a mixing bowl. Season with salt and pepper, then add the vinegar and olive oil and mix well. Leave to marinate at room temperature for at least 30 minutes or longer, if preparing as part of the feast.

2 Bring a large saucepan of salted water to the boil, drop in the spaghetti and cook for 11 minutes, until al dente. Drain the pasta in a colander and add the tomato mixture to the empty spaghetti pan, using the residual heat to warm the tomatoes through. Tip the spaghetti back into the pan, add half the pesto and mix. Serve with the remaining pesto drizzled on top and some olive oil.

6 Asparagus tortilla

- 75ml (2½fl oz) olive oil
- 1 large white Spanish onion, cut into 2cm (¾in) cubes
- 1 garlic clove, finely chopped
- 750g (1lb 10oz) cooked asparagus spears (see step 1, page 96)
- 8 large free-range eggs
- 150g (5½oz) Grana Padano or mild Cheddar cheese, finely grated
- 2 tbsp pine nuts
- salt and pepper

Serves 4–6 | Vegetarian

1 Heat the olive oil in a large frying pan, add the onion and cook over a gentle heat until translucent, stirring occasionally. Add the garlic and continue frying for 3 minutes. Add the asparagus pieces, increase the heat to medium-high and shake the pan to combine.

2 Break the eggs into a bowl and whisk well, seasoning with salt and pepper. Pour the eggs into the pan and reduce the heat to medium. Preheat the grill to high. As the eggs set in the pan, use a spatula to loosen around the edges. Sprinkle the cheese and scatter over the pine nuts.

3 When the tortilla is nearly cooked, after about 4 minutes, put the pan under the grill (turning the handle away from the heat source) to cook the top. Grill for 6 minutes until golden brown and firm, then give the pan a good shake to release it. Slide the tortilla on to a board, sprinkle with paprika and cut into wedges to serve.

As I pulled this very tart out of the oven, a great band I know, who were on tour, pulled up to play a gig in our kitchen. They went mad for it. If you can't find truffled goats' cheese, use any strong cheese and drizzle a teaspoon of truffle oil in when making the dough.

Leek tart with truffled goats' cheese

- **1 quantity Shortcrust pastry (*see* page 296)**
- **150g (5¹/₂oz) truffled goats' cheese, broken into small pieces**
- **12 leeks, white parts only**
- **70g (2¹/₂oz) butter**
- **4 free-range eggs**
- **100ml (3¹/₂fl oz) double cream**
- **freshly grated nutmeg**
- **salt and pepper**

Serves 4–6 | Vegetarian

1   Preheat the oven to 160°C/fan 140°C/gas mark 3. Roll out two-thirds of the pastry on a work surface lightly dusted with flour and use it to line the base of a 25cm (10in) flan tin, leaving a 1–1¹/₂cm (¹/₂ – ⁵/₈in) overhang. Roll out the remaining pastry for the lid of the tart. Scatter the cheese into the pastry case.

2   Using a very sharp knife, cut the whites of the leeks in half lengthways. Wash them under cold running water to remove any sand or soil, then drain and slice into 1cm (¹/₂in) pieces. Drop the leeks into a saucepan of salted boiling water and cook for 5 minutes. Drain, refresh under cold running water and drain again.

3   Melt the butter in a saucepan. Add the leeks, stir well and cook over a medium heat for 2–3 minutes, stirring occasionally. Beat the eggs with the cream and pour slowly into the leeks with the pan off the heat, stirring constantly. Season with nutmeg, salt and pepper to taste.

4   Pour the leek mixture into the tart case, and brush the overhanging pastry with beaten egg. Place the lid on top of the tart case, fold in the overhanging pastry and press down around the edge to seal. Cut a slit in the centre to let the steam escape. Bake for 40 minutes and serve hot.

This dish is a lovely afternoon snack. Add as much Worcestershire sauce as you can – it cuts brilliantly across the sweet leeks.

Leeks on toast with cheese & Worcestershire sauce

- 500g (1lb 2oz) leeks, white parts only
- 50g (1³/₄oz) butter
- 250ml (9fl oz) Cheesy béchamel sauce (*see* page 176)
- 2 tbsp Worcestershire sauce
- 4 slices of bread
- 150g (5¹/₂oz) Cheddar cheese, grated
- salt and pepper

Serves 2–4 | Vegetarian

1   Using a very sharp knife, cut the whites of the leeks lengthways into quarters. Wash them under cold running water to remove any sand or soil, then finely chop them.

2   Melt the butter in a saucepan, add the leeks and a pinch of salt and cook over a medium heat for 10 minutes, until they are soft and translucent, stirring occasionally – cooking them gently in this way helps to bring out their sweetness, and adding a pinch of salt to them at this stage also really enhances their flavour. Add both sauces and mix well. Preheat the grill to medium.

3   When the leek mixture is hot, toast the bread lightly on one side only under the grill, then turn the slices over and spoon the leek mixture on to the untoasted side. Sprinkle the Cheddar on top and put the toast back under the grill to colour the cheese a lovely golden brown. Serve hot with your favourite pickle.

For the best texture in this dish,
keep the leeks in fairly large pieces.

Buttered leeks with thyme & white wine

– 1kg (2lb 4oz) leeks, pale green and
   white parts only
– 150g (5½oz) butter
– 250ml (9fl oz) medium-dry white wine
– 2 tbsp thyme leaves
– salt and pepper

Serves 4–6 | Vegetarian

1   Cut the leeks into 6cm (2½in) pieces and leave to soak in cold water for 30 minutes to remove any sand or soil.

2   Drain the leeks. Put them into a saucepan with the other ingredients, season with salt and pepper and bring to the boil. Reduce the heat and simmer for 25 minutes, until all the liquid has evaporated. Check the seasoning and serve hot.

If there is one vegetable I would like more people to eat, it is the delicious and underrated fennel – and this is a good recipe for introducing people to the world of fennel. You can serve this dish al dente, but I like to cook the fennel for as long as possible.

Braised fennel with fennel seeds

- 4 fennel bulbs, trimmed and fronds reserved
- 75ml (2½fl oz) olive oil, plus extra for drizzling
- 2 garlic cloves
- 2 tbsp fennel seeds
- 1 unwaxed lemon
- 750ml (1¼ pints) warm Vegetable stock (*see* page 297)
- salt and pepper

Serves 4–6 | Vegetarian

1   Discard any tough outer leaves on the fennel, then cut each bulb into eighths.

2   Heat the olive oil in a heavy-based saucepan, add the whole garlic cloves and fennel seeds and cook over a medium heat for 6–8 minutes, until the garlic turns a pale golden brown. Add the fennel pieces, stir well and cook over a medium-high heat for 5 minutes, or until they begin to turn golden brown, stirring frequently. Grate the rind of the lemon directly into the pan and continue to cook. Don't stir too much at this point, as you want the fennel to colour, but keep an eye on it and stir once to prevent it catching. When the fennel begins to darken, season with salt and pepper.

3   Add a ladle of the warm vegetable stock and allow it to evaporate and be absorbed. Continue this process until the stock is all used up, then cover the pan with a lid and reduce the heat to low. Cook for 15 minutes more if you want the fennel al dente, or for 20 minutes if you prefer it completely tender. Just before you serve the dish, chop the fennel fronds and drop them in, then drizzle in a little more olive oil.

Frying coated fennel in olive oil brings a delicious crunch and seals in the lovely aniseed flavour.
It's a great way to make the most of any breadcrumbs you might have to hand. You could use this idea for most types of vegetable.

Breadcrumbed fennel slices with lime & chilli dressing

- 4 fennel bulbs, trimmed and fronds removed
- 2 free-range eggs
- 3 tbsp milk
- 150g (5½oz) plain flour
- 250g (9oz) fresh white breadcrumbs
- 100ml (3½fl oz) light olive oil
- salt and pepper
- lime wedges, to serve

Lime & chilli dressing
- juice and finely grated rind of 1 lime
- 1 fresh red chilli, finely diced
- 1 large banana shallot
- 150ml (¼ pint) light olive oil
- 2 tsp caster sugar
- 50 ml (2fl oz) white wine vinegar
- 1 tsp mustard
- 50 ml (2 fl oz) olive oil
- salt and pepper

Serves 4–6 | Vegetarian

1   First make the lime dressing. Put the lime juice and zest in a bowl. Chop the chilli and add to the bowl, then finely chop the shallots and add to the bowl. Add the olive oil, a bit at a time, mixing vigorously with a balloon whisk, to bruise the chilli and shallot and release the flavour. Add the sugar and white wine vinegar, continuing to mix well. Transfer to a dipping bowl.

2   Discard any tough outer leaves on the fennel, then cut each bulb into eighths. Drop the fennel into a saucepan of salted boiling water and cook for 5 minutes. Drain and leave to cool to room temperature.

3   Lightly beat the eggs and milk together in a mixing bowl and season with a little salt and pepper. Put the flour on a plate and season lightly. Put the breadcrumbs on a separate plate. First, lightly dust the blanched fennel with the seasoned flour, then coat with the egg and finally the breadcrumbs. Set aside on a plate.

4   Heat the olive oil in a frying pan over a medium heat. Add the breadcrumbed fennel and fry gently for about 4–6 minutes, until golden brown on the underside, then turn over and cook for another 4–6 minutes, until browned on the other side. Serve with lime wedges, along with the lime dressing for dipping.

I've been serving up ceviche for years, but it amazes me how few people cook this fantastic dish. You can use other types of fish as long as it is super-fresh. This recipe is a winner every time.

Fennel & salmon ceviche

- 400ml (14fl oz) freshly squeezed
  lemon juice
- 150ml (¼ pint) olive oil, plus extra
  to serve
- 1 fresh green chilli, thinly sliced
  into rings
- 2 shallots, very thinly sliced into rings
- 500g (1lb 2oz) skinless salmon fillet,
  pin-boned and thinly sliced
- 2 fennel bulbs, trimmed and
  fronds removed
- 1 tsp herb vinegar
- 1 tsp caster sugar
- 1 tsp finely chopped mint
- salt and pepper
- crème fraîche, to serve
- 2 tsp chopped dill, to garnish

Serves 4–6

1   Pour the lemon juice and 75ml (2½fl oz) of the olive oil into a mixing bowl and stir in the chilli and shallots.

2   Arrange the salmon in a shallow, non-metallic dish large enough to hold all the slices. Pour the lemon juice mixture over the fish and season with salt and pepper. Cover with clingfilm and leave to cook in the acidic lemon juice in the refrigerator for 1 hour.

3   Meanwhile, discard any tough outer leaves on the fennel and thinly slice each bulb. Put the fennel in the bowl that you used for the lemon juice mixture. Add the vinegar, sugar and mint and the rest of the olive oil. Mix well, using your fingers.

4   Arrange half of the fennel mixture on a serving platter, then lift the salmon, chilli and shallot out of the marinade and on to the salad, before adding another layer of fennel. Dress with a splash more olive oil and drizzle over some crème fraîche. Serve sprinkled with the chopped dill and a crack of pepper.

I reckon I have cooked a version of this dish every week for the past 20 years. It is the simplest and quickest way to roast potatoes, and the best bits are the crispy edges. You can replace the fennel with just about anything – one of my favourites is red onion.

Fennel & potatoes al forno

- 1kg (2lb 4oz) fennel bulbs, trimmed and fronds removed
- 1kg (2lb 4oz) Linska or other medium-sized waxy potatoes, scrubbed
- 4 shallots, thinly sliced
- 2 garlic cloves, thinly sliced
- 1/2 bunch of thyme
- 75ml (2 1/2fl oz) extra virgin olive oil, plus extra for drizzling
- salt and pepper

Serves 4–6 | Vegetarian

1   Preheat the oven to 190°C/fan 170°C/gas mark 5. Line a large roasting tray with baking parchment. Discard any tough outer leaves on the fennel, then cut each bulb lengthways into slices 2cm (3/4in) thick. Cut the potatoes lengthways into thick 1cm (1/2in) slices.

2   Put the fennel and potatoes into a mixing bowl with the shallots, garlic, thyme and olive oil, season with salt and pepper and mix together well. Spread the mixture out on the prepared tray. Drizzle over a little more olive oil and roast for 40 minutes.

Red onion & potatoes al forno

Replace the fennel with 1 large red onion. Roughly chop it and place in a bowl with the potatoes, prepared as above. Add all the other ingredients plus 4 tablespoons balsamic vinegar, mix well and cook as in step 2.

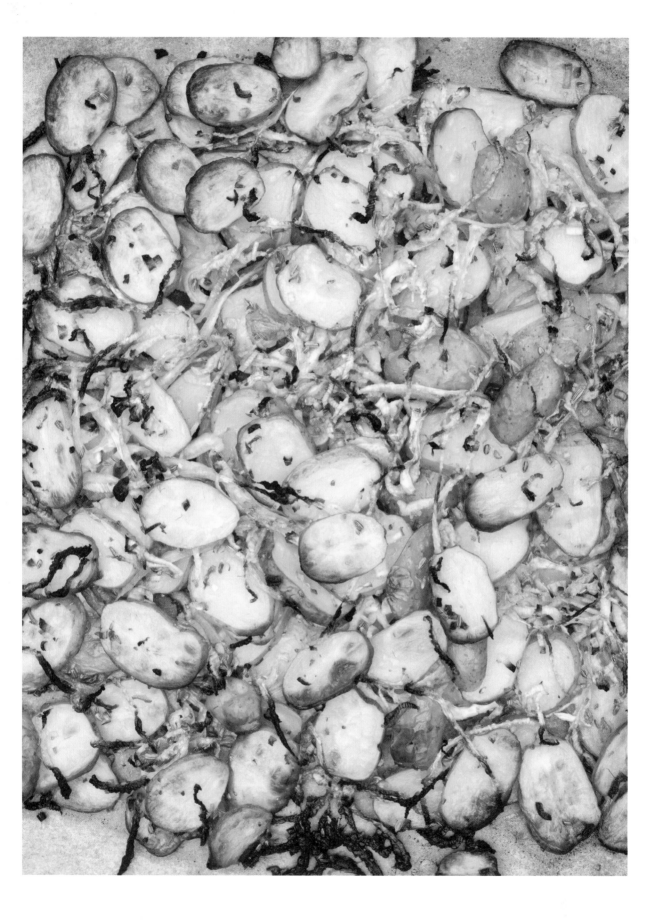

Fennel and orange go really well together: each gives the other the support needed to bring out its flavour, and the grapes add a Mediterranean flavour. There are Asian versions of this dish too, with ginger, garlic and sesame in place of the parsley, mint and sunflower seeds.

Fennel salad with oranges, grapes & sunflower seeds

- 2 fennel bulbs, trimmed and fronds removed
- 2 large navel oranges
- 300g (10½oz) red grapes
- 1 small white onion
- 2 tbsp chopped flat leaf parsley
- 2 tbsp chopped mint
- 50ml (2fl oz) olive oil
- 2 tbsp cider vinegar
- 3 tbsp sunflower seeds
- salt and pepper

Serves 4–6 | Vegetarian

1   Discard any tough outer leaves on the fennel, then cut the bulbs into thin slices. Using a knife, peel the oranges and remove any white pith, then cut into discss 2cm (¾in) thick. Cut the grapes in half and remove any pips. Thinly slice the onion.

2   Put all the prepared ingredients into a mixing bowl and add the parsley and mint. Add the olive oil and vinegar, season with salt and pepper and mix very well – you can be a little robust with the mixing; the orange and fennel are fine when bruised together.

3   Heat a dry frying pan over a medium heat, tip in the sunflower seeds, then shake the pan until they start to crackle and toast, but watch carefully so that they don't burn.

4   Arrange the salad in a serving dish and sprinkle the warm sunflower seeds over the top.

Eating raw, crunchy vegetables is a lovely way to get all your essential vitamins and minerals. I've dropped some capers, pomegranate seeds and pine nuts into this salad to add texture and even more goodness.

Kohl slaw

- **400g kohlrabi**
- **200g carrots**
- **200g white cabbage**
- **100ml Homemade mayonnaise (*see* page 297)**
- **2 tbsp capers in vinegar, drained**
- **4 tbsp pomegranate seeds**
- **2 tbsp pine nuts**
- **salt and pepper**

Serves 4–6 | Vegetarian

1   Slice the kohlrabi and carrots into very thin matchsticks. Slice the cabbage very thinly too.

2   Put all the vegetables into a mixing bowl. Add the mayonnaise, season with salt and pepper and mix together well. Sprinkle in half the capers, pomegranate seeds and pine nuts and mix again, taking care not to crush the pomegranate seeds.

3   Divide the kohl slaw between serving dishes, then sprinkle over the remaining capers, seeds and nuts.

The firmness of the pumpkin makes this dish really substantial, but it doesn't matter how much you make – it will all get eaten. The cheese pastry on this pie is super-wicked: make a double batch and use it to make cheese biscuits another day.

Kohlrabi pie with root vegetables

- 400g (14oz) kohlrabi, cut into 2cm (¾in) cubes
- 200g (7oz) celeriac, cut into 2cm (¾in) cubes
- 200g (7oz) Crown Prince or other firm pumpkin, deseeded and cut into 2cm (¾in) cubes
- 200g (7oz) carrots, cut into 2cm (¾in) cubes
- 200g (7oz) potato, cut into 2cm (¾in) cubes
- 1 litre (1¾ pints) milk
- ½ tsp freshly grated nutmeg
- 3 tbsp rosemary leaves, half of them finely chopped
- 200g (7oz) butter
- 1 white onion, finely chopped
- 200g (7oz) plain flour
- 3 tbsp Dijon mustard
- 50g (1¾oz) Cheddar cheese, grated
- 1 quantity Cheese pastry (*see* page 296)
- 1 beaten egg, to glaze
- salt and pepper

Serves 4–6 | Vegetarian

1 Put all the vegetable cubes into a saucepan, cover well with cold water and season with salt. Bring to the boil, then reduce the heat and simmer for 30–35 minutes, until just tender. Drain well in a colander, then leave to drain further on kitchen paper.

2 While the vegetables are cooking, make the sauce. Warm the milk, nutmeg and whole rosemary leaves together in a saucepan. In a separate saucepan, melt the butter, add the onion and a pinch of salt and cook over a gentle heat for about 10 minutes until soft, stirring occasionally – adding a pinch of salt at this stage will prevent the onion from colouring. Add the flour and stir well, then slowly start to add the warm milk, keeping the mixture smooth by stirring constantly and not adding too much milk at once. Season with salt and pepper, add the mustard and chopped rosemary and set aside.

3 Preheat the oven to 190°C/fan 170°C/gas mark 5. Put all the drained vegetables into another large mixing bowl and add the Cheddar cheese. Pour in the onion sauce and mix lightly to avoid squashing the vegetables. Tip the whole mixture into an ovenproof dish about 25 x 20cm (10 x 8in). Roll out the pastry on a lightly floured work surface and cover the dish, crimping around the edges. Cut a slit in the centre of the pie to let the steam escape and brush the pastry with beaten egg to glaze. Bake for 30 minutes, or until the pastry is golden brown. Serve hot.

Poached celery heart is brilliant on its own, but combining it with horseradish makes it outstanding. Traditionally served with boiled veg or meat, it would also work with salmon or some roast celeriac.

Poached celery hearts with roast chicken & horseradish crème fraîche

- **6 boneless free-range chicken thighs, skin on**
- **2 tbsp olive oil**
- **1 tsp thyme leaves**
- **1.5 litres (2¾ pints) Vegetable stock (*see* page 297)**
- **6 bay leaves**
- **6 celery hearts, divided in two lengthways**
- **150ml (¼ pint) crème fraîche**
- **2 tbsp red wine vinegar**
- **2 tbsp olive oil**
- **4 tbsp peeled and grated fresh horseradish, very finely chopped**
- **salt and pepper**

Serves 6

1   Preheat the oven to 180°C/fan 160°C/gas mark 4. Put the chicken thighs in a roasting tray, drizzle on the olive oil, then sprinkle the thyme leaves evenly across them. Season with salt and pepper and roast in the oven for 25 minutes.

2   Meanwhile, put the vegetable stock into a saucepan and bring to the boil, then reduce the heat to a simmer. Add the bay leaves to the stock and season lightly with salt and pepper. Drop the celery hearts into the stock and simmer for 15–20 minutes, until the celery is tender but still firm to the bite.

3   Spoon the crème fraîche into a bowl and add the vinegar and olive oil. Add the horseradish and mix together well. When the chicken is cooked, serve on plates with the poached celery hearts alongside and a little of the stock from the celery poured over the top. Spoon on the horseradish cream to finish.

This is great served simply with crusty bread and butter, and perhaps a slice of ham.

Celery salad with walnuts, Stilton & apple

- 2 heads of celery, tops and tough outer sticks removed
- 200g (7oz) walnut halves
- 2 russet apples
- 4 heads of Baby Gem lettuce, leaves separated
- 3 tbsp Homemade mayonnaise (*see* page 297)
- 100ml (3¹/₂fl oz) House dressing (*see* page 297)
- 150g (5¹/₂oz) Stilton cheese
- salt and pepper

Serves 4–6 | **Vegetarian**

1 Preheat the oven to 180°C/fan 160°C/gas mark 4. Chop the celery widthways at 1cm (¹/₂in) intervals. Wash and drain the celery, then put it into a mixing bowl.

2 Spread the walnuts on a baking sheet and toast in the oven for 12–15 minutes. Remove and leave to cool. Meanwhile, core and chop the apples into pieces to match the celery, then add to the bowl along with the lettuce. Crumble in the Stilton, then add the walnuts. Spoon in the mayonnaise and drizzle in the dressing, then season lightly with salt and pepper. Mix well and serve immediately.

Celery lends itself really well to smoked flavour combinations. You can get smoked cheese in lots of different styles, and I'm a big fan of smoked salt and smoked garlic – both of which you could use in this dish.

Cream of celery soup with smoked cheese

- 50g (1³/₄oz) butter
- 50ml (2fl oz) olive oil
- 1 white onion, chopped
- 1 garlic clove
- 2 heads of celery
- 1 thyme sprig
- 1 large potato, cut into 2–3cm
  (³/₄–1¹/₄in) cubes
- 1 litre (1³/₄ pints) hot Vegetable stock
  (*see* page 297)
- 150ml (¹/₄ pint) double cream
- 2 tsp celery salt
- 100g (3¹/₂oz) smoked cheese,
  cut into small cubes
- salt and pepper
- toasted crusty bread, to serve

Serves 4–6 | Vegetarian

1   Melt the butter with the olive oil in a large saucepan. Add the onion and a pinch salt and cook over a medium heat for 4–5 minutes, stirring occasionally. Add the whole garlic clove and cook for 5 minutes, until softened. Meanwhile, chop the celery, including the leaves, widthways at 1cm (¹/₂in) intervals. Wash and drain the celery. Reserve a few leaves for garnishing.

2   Add the celery and thyme to the pan of onions and cook gently for 5 minutes, stirring occasionally. Stir in the potato, then pour in the hot stock and season with pepper. Bring to the boil, then reduce the heat and simmer for 10 minutes, or until the potato is tender. Leave to cool a little, then transfer to a blender in batches and blend until smooth. Pour into a clean saucepan and stir in the cream and celery salt. Check the seasoning and reheat gently. Ladle the soup into bowls, then drop in the smoked cheese cubes and the reserved celery leaves. Serve with toasted crusty bread, if you like.

I really wanted to put this type of classic meal into the book – it is so totally retro that it's cool. I would prepare this for a special occasion, but you can take each component and serve it any time. It contains meat and fish, but without the veg elements it wouldn't be anything like as exciting. I learned to cook the Trellis of salmon & salsify from the Roux brothers. The technique is worth experimenting with – you can use different vegetables and fish if you want to. The Chilled lettuce soup is from the Dorchester hotel in London, and the Shredded raddicchio & green chilli with carpaccio is inspired by my River Café days. The Buttered potatoes, broad beans & peas are a classic combination – I find myself pulling the dish over and eating straight from the bowl. Serve with ciabbatta, butter and some finely chopped green chilli in olive oil.

Classic

1 Chilled lettuce soup with champagne & caviar

- 50g (1³/₄oz) butter
- 1 large white onion, fairly finely chopped
- 2 small potatoes, finely chopped
- 250ml (9fl oz) champagne
- 3 heads of Cos (Romaine) lettuce, roughly chopped
- 1 litre (1³/₄ pints) hot Vegetable stock (*see* page 297)
- 250ml (9fl oz) double cream
- 6 tsp caviar
- salt and pepper

Serves 4–6

1   Melt the butter in a saucepan, add the onion and cook over a medium heat for 5 minutes without colouring, stirring frequently. Add the potatoes and cook for 7 minutes, stirring frequently. Pour in the champagne and allow the alcohol to evaporate before adding the lettuce. Stir well, then pour in the hot stock and bring to a simmer. Cook for about 8 minutes, or until the potatoes are soft.

2   Leave the soup to cool for a few minutes, then transfer to a blender in batches and blend until smooth, adding the cream and seasoning as you do so. Pour all the blended soup into a clean saucepan and reheat gently. Serve the soup in cups or bowls, each topped with a spoonful of caviar.

2 Shredded raddicchio & green chilli with beef carpaccio

- 1 head of radicchio
- 600g (1lb 5oz) piece of beef fillet, trimmed of any sinew or fat
- 3 tbsp olive oil, plus extra for drizzling
- 1 fresh green chilli, deseeded and chopped
- juice of 1 lemon
- sea salt and pepper

Serves 4–6

1   Discard the outer leaves from the radicchio, cut the head into quarters and reserve in the refrigerator. Make sure the fillet of beef is cold and season with salt and pepper. Heat a heavy-based frying pan until very hot, add the olive oil and then seal the beef on all sides to achieve an even, dark golden surface – the inside will be still red. This will take about 5 minutes. Set the beef aside to cool, then return it to the refrigerator for 30 minutes.

2   Put the meat on a chopping board, placing it so the grain runs from left to right. Using a very sharp knife, cut very thin slices across the grain – this is key to ensuring that each mouthful is perfectly tender. Arrange the slices to cover a serving plate, then lightly season with sea salt and pepper and drizzle with olive oil.

3   Cut the radicchio quarters as thinly as possible to create thin strips and sprinkle them over the seasoned carpaccio. Chop the chilli and sprinkle that over the plate. Drizzle over more olive oil, sprinkle with a touch more sea salt and serve immediately.

3 Buttered potatoes, broad beans & peas

- 750g (1lb 10oz) Linska or other medium-sized waxy potatoes, scrubbed
- 300g (10½oz) broad beans, podded weight
- 300g (10½oz) peas, podded weight
- 2 tbsp finely chopped mint leaves
- 75g (2³/₄oz) butter, plus extra to serve
- salt and pepper

Serves 4–6 | Vegetarian

1   Put the potatoes into the bottom tier of a steamer, preferably a bamboo one, and steam for 20 minutes, until cooked but still with a slight bite to them. Put the broad beans and peas into the second tier, place this on top of the potato tier and steam for 5 minutes until cooked.

2   Sprinkle the mint on to both tiers and season with salt and pepper. Cut up the butter, then put it on to the broad beans and peas and allow it to drip down on to the potatoes. Serve together with an extra knob of butter on top.

4 Trellis of salmon & salsify with cucumber beurre blanc

- juice of 1 lemon
- 1 handful of parsley stalks, crushed
- 700g (1lb 9oz) salsify
- 950g (2lb 2oz) salmon fillet
- 1 cucumber
- olive oil, for drizzling
- salt and pepper

Beurre blanc
- 4 shallots, finely chopped
- 1 tsp white peppercorns
- 2 bay leaves
- 200ml (7fl oz) white wine vinegar
- 200ml (7fl oz) medium-dry white wine
- 75ml (2½fl oz) double cream
- 250g (9oz) cold butter, cut into small cubes

Serves 6

1   Add the lemon juice, parsley and some salt to a bowl of cold water. Working quickly, peel the salsify, then drop them into the prepared water to prevent them from turning brown. Bring a saucepan of salted water to the boil, add the salsify and cook for 7–8 minutes, until they are just tender. Drain and cool in cold water. Cut the salsify in half lengthways and reserve in cold water.

2   To create the trellises, cut the salmon fillet into 24 strips. Line a large baking sheet with baking parchment and arrange 4 salmon strips side by side, then weave 3 drained salsify strips horizontally, in and out of the salmon strips. Repeat the process to make another 5 trellises. Reserve in the refrigerator.

3   Peel the cucumber, discarding the green skin, then keep peeling the flesh into thin strips until you reach the seeds, which you also discard. Put the cucumber strips into a sieve, sprinkle lightly with salt and leave for 20 minutes to allow the excess liquid to drain away.

4   Meanwhile, preheat the oven to 180°C/fan 160°C/gas mark 4 and make the beurre blanc. Put the shallots into a saucepan, add the peppercorns, bay leaves, vinegar and wine and cook over a medium heat until the liquid has reduced by two-thirds. Add the cream and bring to the boil, then reduce the heat to low. Add the butter, no more than 2 cubes at a time, whisking constantly and adding more only once the cubes in the sauce have melted. Strain through a fine sieve into a clean pan and keep warm but without boiling. Squeeze the cucumber dry, add to the beurre blanc and stir to combine.

5   Lightly season the trellises with salt and pepper and drizzle over a little olive oil, then place in the oven for 8–9 minutes. To serve, spoon the beurre blanc on to serving plates and carefully place a trellis on top. Serve warm.

This is so, so, so simple – brilliant by itself or delicious served on toasted ciabbata. And it's fine to experiment – try adding a couple of handfuls of whole spring onions to the tray before roasting. You can use the discarded asparagus stalks for the recipe on the following page.

Asparagus al forno with cherry tomatoes & basil

- 1.4kg (3lb 1oz) asparagus spears, woody stalks removed
- 500g (1lb 2oz) cherry tomatoes
- 2 garlic cloves, chopped
- 4 tbsp roughly chopped basil
- 75ml (2½fl oz) olive oil
- salt and pepper

Serves 4–6 | Vegetarian

1   Preheat the oven to 190°C/fan 170°C/gas mark 5 and line a roasting tray with baking parchment.

2   Put the asparagus spears into a large mixing bowl. Add the tomatoes, garlic and basil, drizzle in the olive oil and season with salt and pepper. Mix well, making sure that everything is covered in oil and seasoning. Tip on to the prepared tray and roast for 15–20 minutes – checking after 15. The tomatoes and asparagus should be tender but not soggy.

Asparagus & peas al forno

Follow the recipe above and prepare the ingedients in exactly the same way, adding a couple of handfuls of fresh peas in their pods to the mixture.

Chefs always find ways to make the most of their food and we can all benefit from some of their tricks to eliminate waste and even cut down on our own food bills. Next time you're making an asparagus dish, save the discarded trimmings and make a batch of this soup.

Waste not asparagus soup

- 750g (1lb 10oz) leftover asparagus stalks
- 50ml (2fl oz) olive oil
- 1 head of celery, trimmed and cut into 2cm (3/4in) cubes
- 1 large white onion, cut into 2cm (3/4in) cubes
- 1 large potato, cut into 2cm (3/4in) cubes
- 2 garlic cloves, roughly chopped
- 1.5 litres (2¾ pints) Vegetable stock (*see* page 297)
- 150ml (¼ pint) double cream
- lemon juice, to taste
- olive oil, for drizzling
- salt and pepper

Serves 4–6 | Vegetarian

1   Slice the asparagus stalks, discarding the toughest woody bits. Set aside.

2   Heat the olive oil in a saucepan, add the celery, onion and potato and cook over a medium heat for 5 minutes without colouring, stirring occasionally. Add the garlic and season with salt and pepper, then stir and cook gently for a further 5 minutes. Add most of the asparagus pieces, reserving about 4 tablespoons for garnish, mix well and then add the stock. Bring to the boil, then reduce and simmer for 10 minutes, or until the potatoes are tender.

3   Increase the heat again and bring the soup to the boil, then stir in the cream and turn off the heat. Leave to cool a little, then transfer to a blender in batches and blend until smooth. Pour into a clean saucepan, add the reserved asparagus and reheat gently. Check the seasoning and squeeze in a little lemon juice. Serve hot in bowls with a drizzle of olive oil.

I love this salad – it's a sure sign that summer is on its way. Peas, asparagus and broad beans are superb when they are picked fresh and young. Don't cook them for too long and do chop those shallots superfine.

Asparagus salad with peas, broad beans & mint

- 1kg (2lb 4oz) asparagus, woody stalks removed
- 500g (1lb 2oz) broad beans, podded
- 500g (1lb 2oz) peas, podded
- 2 shallots, finely diced
- 3 tbsp roughly chopped mint
- 4 tbsp House dressing (*see* page 297)

Serves 4–6 | Vegetarian

1   Cook the asparagus spears in a large saucepan of salted boiling water for about 6 minutes, until tender. Drain and leave to cool.

2   Meanwhile, blanch the broad beans in a large saucepan of salted boiling water for about 2 minutes, adding the peas after about 30 seconds. Drain and leave to cool.

3   Put the cooled asparagus into a large bowl with the broad beans and peas. Add the shallots and half the chopped mint and mix together. Drizzle in the dressing and mix together again. Serve topped with the remaining mint.

Asparagus salad with egg & bacon

Prepare and make the salad as above. While it is cooling, preheat the grill and cook 2 slices of streaky bacon per person for 4–6 minutes, turning once. Meanwhile, melt a little butter in a frying pan and fry a couple of eggs per person over a low heat. When cooked, slide on to the salad and top with the bacon.

Samphire and spaetzle is a dish I wish everyone would try. It is far from complicated to cook, and is a great alternative to the traditional 'two-veg' part of meals. Get samphire while it's young and in season. Red mullet is a delicious and sustainable fish – well worth trying.

Samphire & spaetzle with chilli & red mullet

- **450g (1lb) samphire**
- **3 tbsp olive oil**
- **1 fresh red chilli, finely chopped**
- **lemon juice, to taste**
- **12 red mullet fillets**
- **salt and pepper**
- **6 lemon cheeks, to serve** (*see* page 44)

Spaetzle
- **400g (14oz) plain flour**
- **4 free-range eggs**
- **200ml (7fl oz) double cream**
- **salt and pepper**

Serves 6

1   First make the spaetzle. Put the flour into a large mixing bowl and make a well in the centre. Break the eggs into the well and mix, using a stiff whisk, until the mixture becomes too thick to whisk. Add the cream, season with salt and pepper and continue whisking until smooth and elastic – the consistency should be like a thick pancake batter. Put a large saucepan of salted water on to boil.

2   Now tip the mixture on to a lightweight board. Using a palette knife, start cutting the dough into very small strips and dropping them into the boiling water. They will instantly sink to the bottom, but float to the surface when cooked. Continue cutting and adding strips to the pan until there is no room left. When all the spaetzle have floated to the surface, after about 2 minutes, lift out with a small sieve and drop them into iced water. Repeat this process until the dough is used up.

3   Prepare the samphire just before cooking it by picking off any hard pieces at the base of the stalks, then wash in cold water and drain. Blanch immediately in a pan of boiling water for 2 minutes, then refresh it in cold water and drain again.

4   Drain the spaetzle well and pat dry with kitchen paper. Heat 2 tablespoons of the olive oil in a frying pan, add the spaetzle and cook over a medium-high heat for 6–8 minutes, until golden brown and crisp, stirring occasionally with a wooden spoon. Add the samphire, mix for a minute to heat it through, then add the chilli, lemon juice and seasoning. Meanwhile, heat the remaining olive oil in a separate frying pan, add the red mullet fillets skin-side down, and cook for 4 minutes. Turn them over and cook for a further 2 minutes – no more, as red mullet very easily overcooks.

5   Divide the spaetzle and samphire mixture on to serving plates alongside the mullet. Serve with lemon cheeks.

As a young chef, I spent weeks preparing samphire when the season started, and my fingers had turned a deep green by the end of it. Huge boxes used to arrive at the back door of the kitchen, and you had to prepare it pretty quickly, as it deteriorates very fast. The boxes smelt of the sea, with a rich minerally top note. We served samphire with nearly every fish dish we sent out. I can't think of a better accompaniment.

Samphire with spinach & lettuce

- 250g (9oz) bunched spinach
- 250g (9oz) samphire
- 250g (9oz) Baby Gem lettuce
- 3 tbsp virgin olive oil, plus extra for drizzling
- juice of 1 lemon
- salt and pepper

Serves 4–6 | Vegetarian

1   Put 3 separate saucepans of salted water on to boil. Meanwhile, prepare the greens. Wash the spinach well in cold water and cut off the stalks. Reserve both the leaves and stalks in cold water. Pick off any hard pieces at the base of the samphire stalks, then wash them well and reserve in cold water. Discard any damaged outer leaves from the lettuce, then also wash well and reserve in cold water.

2   Drain the lettuce, add to the first pan that comes to the boil and cook for 3 minutes. Drain and place in a large mixing bowl. Drain and add the spinach leaves and stalks to the second pan of boiling water. When tender – it should take no longer than 3 minutes to cook – drain in a colander, then add it to the lettuce. Put the samphire into the last pan of boiling water and cook for just 2 minutes or so, until tender. Drain and add it to the lettuce and samphire.

3   Add the olive oil to the bowl with most of the lemon juice and season with salt and pepper. Mix well and arrange on a serving plate. Sprinkle with a little more salt and the remaining lemon juice and drizzle with extra olive oil.

Lettuce
Spinach
Rocket
Sorrel
Radicchio
Chicory
Kale
Cabbage
Cauliflower
Broccoli
Artichoke

Leaves
&
Flowers

The story of how this salad was created leaves me smiling. It is claimed that Caesar Cardini, an Italian chef working in Tijuana, Mexico, was low on food and put the salad together with what he had in his kitchen cupboards. The Worcestershire sauce he added was at the time a cough syrup, often found lurking on back shelves in pharmacies. To me, this illustrates the freakish nature of food and how strange combinations often work brilliantly.

Chicken Caesar salad

- **2 free-range chicken breasts**
- **olive oil, for drizzling**
- **1 French bread stick**
- **3 free-range eggs, hard boiled**
- **2 heads of Cos (Romaine) lettuce**
- **100g (3¹/₂oz) salted capers, soaked in cold water for 10 minutes, drained and squeezed dry**
- **100g (3¹/₂oz) Parmesan cheese shavings**

Dressing
- **4 anchovy fillets**
- **75g (2³/₄oz) Parmesan cheese, finely grated**
- **2 free-range egg yolks**
- **2 tbsp Worcestershire sauce**
- **1 garlic clove**
- **juice of 1 lemon**
- **200ml (7fl oz) olive oil**
- **salt and pepper**

Serves 4–6

1   Preheat the oven to 190°C/fan 170°C/gas mark 5. For the dressing, put all the ingredients except the olive oil into a blender and blend until you have a smooth paste. With the motor still running, drizzle in the oil, not too much to start with, but adding it more rapidly as the mixture thickens. Check for seasoning and set aside.

2   Put the chicken breasts in a roasting tray, drizzle with a little olive oil and sprinkle with salt and pepper. Roast for 25 minutes. Cut the bread into 2cm (³/₄in) chunks, spread out on a baking sheet and drizzle with olive oil. Bake for 6–8 minutes, until golden brown, turning once or twice during cooking, then leave to cool. Shell the eggs and cut into quarters. Separate the lettuce leaves, trim, then wash and dry in a salad spinner.

3   Cut the chicken into large chunks and put into a large bowl. Add the croutons, capers and the eggs. Pour in most of the dressing and delicately mix together. Plate the salad, sprinkle over the Parmesan shavings and drizzle with the last of the dressing.

Classic Caesar salad

For the classic, vegetarian version, omit the chicken and add 2 ripe avocados cut into chunks when you add the eggs. Dress and serve as above.

Most people think of lettuce as a salad ingredient. Well, here's a recipe that shows lettuce is excellent cooked.

Braised lettuce with lardons & bay leaf salt

- 250g (9oz) lardons
- 12 heads of Baby Gem lettuce
- 2 tbsp olive oil
- 1 celery heart, finely chopped
- 200ml (7fl oz) medium-dry white wine
- 500ml (18fl oz) Vegetable stock (*see* page 297)
- pepper

Bay leaf salt
- 6 tbsp rock salt
- 6 bay leaves

Serves 4–6

1   For the bay leaf salt, put the salt and bay leaves into a blender and blend on high speed until finely ground, without any large crystals or pieces of bay remaining.

2   Place the lardons in a saucepan with just enough water to cover them and bring to the boil. Meanwhile, discard any tough outer leaves from the lettuces, cut the hearts in half and wash well in cold water. Dry well.

3   After 6–8 minutes, drain the lardons and pat dry with kitchen paper. Heat the olive oil in a large frying pan, add the lardons and cook over a medium-high heat until golden brown, stirring frequently. Add the celery and cook, stirring frequently, for 3 minutes, then add the lettuce halves and 1 teaspoon of the bay leaf salt. Mix well and cook for 5 minutes, allowing the lettuce to wilt. Add the wine and cook for 3 minutes, then pour in the stock. Cover the pan with a lid or a circle of baking parchment, reduce the heat to low and cook for 15 minutes. Remove the lid or paper, check for seasoning and serve hot.

This recipe is almost perfect in its simplicity. It is too delicious not to make it almost every week, especially in the summer months when the leaves are young but punchy. So here it is, full of flavour and singing of summer.

Ten-leaf salad

- 1 head of oak leaf lettuce
- 1 head of frisée lettuce
- 1 bunch of wild rocket
- 1 bunch of watercress
- 2 heads of Baby Gem lettuce
- 1 bunch of chervil
- 1/2 bunch of flat leaf parsley
- 1 handful of mint tips
- 1 handful of celery leaves
- 1/2 handful of baby basil leaves
- 300ml (1/2 pint) House dressing (*see* page 297)
- salt and pepper

Serves 4–6 | Vegetarian

1   Prepare a sinkful of cold water and add some ice cubes. Separate the lettuce leaves, discarding any damaged ones, and drop them into the iced water. Check over the rocket and watercress leaves, then add them to the iced water too. Add all the herb leaves to the iced water and leave for 15 minutes to firm up.

2   Drain the leaves, then dry them and place in a large bowl. Season lightly with salt and pepper and drizzle in the dressing. Arrange neatly on side plates or on one large platter and serve.

Eleven- or twelve-leaf salad

Try adding different or extra leaves to this salad: for a super-bitter taste, add some radicchio, curly endive or young dandelion leaves. For a really herby salad, add summer savory, chives and fresh sorrel leaves. My favourite salad is one filled with edible flowers, such as nasturtiums, marigolds or – for a sweet edge – honeysuckle flowers.

Super-fresh, super-colourful and super-cool, this is a great salad to put in front of your friends when they visit for that delicious meal you promised them. I guarantee a summery, refreshing explosion of flavours.

Couscous salad with Iceberg lettuce, tomato & mint

- 500g (1lb 2oz) couscous
- 100ml (3½fl oz) olive oil
- 1 tsp dried red chilli flakes
- 1 head of Iceberg lettuce
- 500g (1lb 2oz) yellow and red tomatoes
- 3 tbsp chopped mint
- 75ml (2½fl oz) herb vinegar
- salt and pepper

Serves 4–6 | Vegetarian

1   Put the couscous into a mixing bowl and pour over enough boiling water to cover to a depth of about 1.5–2cm (5/8–3/4in). Drizzle in 75ml (2½fl oz) of the olive oil, sprinkle over the chilli flakes, then cover the bowl with a lid to seal in the heat and steam. Leave until cool.

2   Discard any damaged leaves from the lettuce and shred the remainder finely. Put the lettuce into a large mixing bowl. Cut the tomatoes into quarters, scoop out the seeds and chop each quarter into thin wedges. Add them to the bowl along with the chopped mint, the remaining olive oil and the vinegar and mix well with your hands.

3   Remove the lid from the couscous bowl and use a fork to fluff up the couscous. Add it to the salad and again mix well with your hands. Season with salt and pepper and serve.

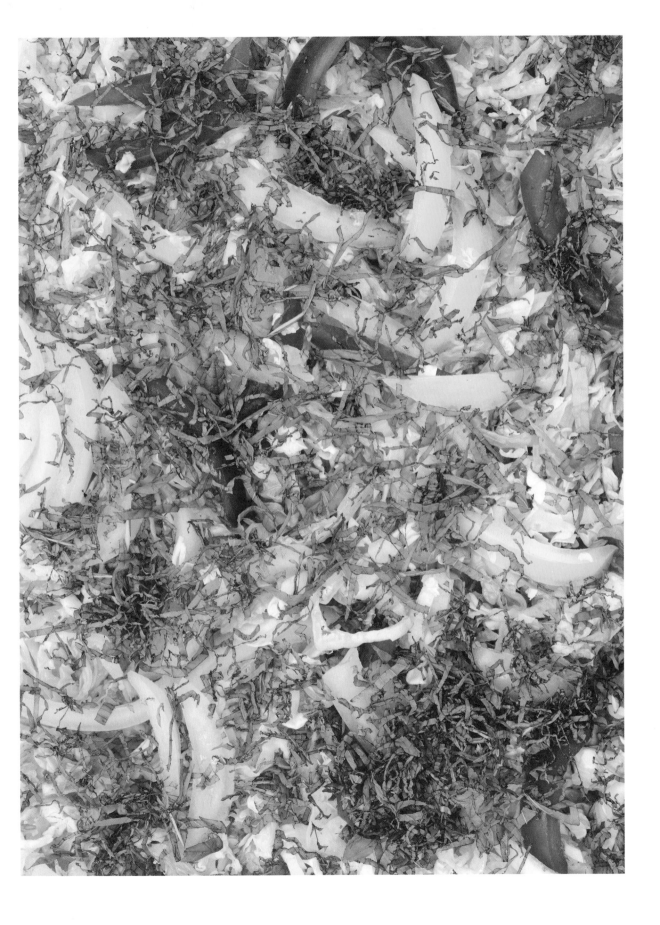

Spinach should be a staple for everyone. It is so easy to cook, by either blanching or steaming, and it takes all sorts of accompaniments.

Creamed spinach with garlic & shallots

- 50ml (2fl oz) olive oil
- 2 shallots, finely chopped
- 2 garlic cloves, finely chopped
- 2kg (4lb 8oz) spinach
- juice of 1 lemon
- 1 tsp Marmite, or ½ tsp salt
- 250ml (9fl oz) double cream
- pepper

Serves 4–6 | Vegetarian

1   Heat the olive oil in a large saucepan and cook the shallots and garlic over a medium heat for 5 minutes, stirring frequently. Meanwhile, wash the spinach well in cold water, drain and shake off the excess water, then roughly chop. Add the spinach to the pan, increase the heat to high and cook, stirring well, until the liquid has evaporated. The spinach will be cooked at this stage.

2   Squeeze in the lemon juice, then add the Marmite and cream. Season with pepper and cook for about 5 minutes, until the cream has slightly thickened. Serve hot – but I've eaten this cold as a leftover, and it is wicked that way too.

Blanched spinach with olive oil & lemon

- 2kg (4lb 8oz) spinach
- juice of 1 lemon
- 50ml (2fl oz) olive oil
- salt and pepper
- lemon wedges, to serve

Serves 6 | Vegetarian

1   Cook the spinach in a large saucepan of salted boiling water for 5 minutes. Meanwhile, squeeze the juice from the lemon into a large mixing bowl. Add the olive oil, season with salt and pepper and whisk together vigorously.

2   Drain the spinach and, while still warm, squeeze the remaining liquid from it. Add the squeezed spinach to the lemon dressing and mix together well. Check the seasoning and serve warm or at room temperature with a wedge of lemon.

The trick here is to keep the pastry thin and the seasoning fairly light as the sun-dried tomatoes and goats' cheese tend to taste salty when cooked.

Spinach & goats' cheese quiche with sun-dried tomatoes

- 340g (11¾oz) Shortcrust pastry (*see* page 296)
- butter, for greasing
- plain flour, for dusting
- 200g (7oz) spinach
- 2 large free-range eggs
- 5 tbsp double cream
- 5 tbsp milk
- 200g (7oz) Parmesan cheese, freshly grated
- 50g (1¾oz) sun-dried tomatoes in oil, drained
- 100g (3½oz) goats' cheese, crumbled
- salt and pepper

To serve
- wild rocket
- 1 quantity House dressing

Serves 4–6 | Vegetarian

1   Grease a flan dish 26cm (10½in) in diameter and dust with flour. Roll out the pastry on a lightly floured surface and line the flan dish with it. Place in the refrigerator and chill for 30 minutes.

2   Meanwhile, cut the spinach into 5cm (2in) pieces. Cook in a saucepan of salted boiling water for 5 minutes, then drain and set aside. Preheat the oven to 200°C/fan 180°C/gas mark 6.

3   Line the pastry case with greaseproof paper and fill with baking beans, then bake for 15 minutes. Remove from the oven, discard the paper and beans and reduce the temperature to 150°C/fan 140°C/gas mark 2. Mix together the eggs, cream, milk, 150g (5½oz) of the Parmesan and salt and pepper. Place the sun-dried tomatoes, goats' cheese and spinach in the cooked pastry case, pour the egg mixture over and sprinkle the rest of the Parmesan on top. Bake in the middle of the oven for 30 minutes, until well risen and golden brown. Serve cut into wedges with lightly dressed wild rocket.

This dish is the type of food I could eat every day. I cook it at home all the time. The kids love it, and we order it when we go out to eat too. Save up your spinach stalks for this one!

Spinach stalks & tofu tempura with dipping sauce

- 1 quantity Tempura batter
  (*see* page 297)
- 500g (1lb 2oz) firm tofu, cut into
  3cm (1¼in) cubes
- 12 clumps of spinach stalks, washed
  and drained
- 3 litres (5¼ pints) vegetable oil,
  for deep-frying

Dipping sauce
- 1 tbsp caster sugar
- 50ml (2fl oz) soy sauce
- 2 tsp dried red chilli flakes
- 75ml (2½fl oz) mirin (rice wine)
- 75ml (2½fl oz) hot Vegetable stock
  (*see* page 297)
- 100g (3½oz) Japanese radish (mouli)

Serves 4–6 | Vegetarian

1   For the sauce, put the sugar into a small saucepan, add the soy sauce, chilli, mirin and hot stock and whisk thoroughly. Peel the radish, then finely grate it into the sauce. Set aside, ready to warm just before serving.

2   Heat the vegetable oil in a deep, heavy-based saucepan to 180°C, or until a cube of bread browns in 30 seconds. Dust the tofu cubes and spinach stalks in flour – this helps the batter to stick to them – and pat off any excess. Dip them into the batter, making sure that every part is covered, and allow any excess batter to drip off. Carefully add the battered stalks and tofu cubes one at a time to the oil, in batches of 3 or 4 pieces, and fry for 3–5 minutes, until a pale golden colour. Don't overfill the pan, otherwise the temperature of the oil will drop and you will be stewing the ingredients rather than deep-frying them. Remove with a slotted spoon and drain on kitchen paper. Pat off any remaining oil. Keep the cooked batches hot while frying the rest. Serve with the warm dipping sauce in bowls on the side.

Seasonal tempura

If you have some batter left over, look around your kitchen for suitable seasonal vegetables to fry – mushrooms are great, as is fennel.

Pasta comes in so many different guises, but rotolo is surely the show-stopper. Get the technique right and you will wow yourself, let alone your mates. You can fill a rotolo with just about anything but this recipe goes for the classic combination of spinach, mushroom, ricotta and nutmeg. You could use button mushrooms if you can't find girolles.

Spinach, mushroom & ricotta rotolo with sage butter

- 150g (5¹/₂oz) butter
- 1 white onion, finely chopped
- 4 tbsp chopped marjoram
- 800g (1lb 12oz) cooked spinach, chopped (*see* page 146)
- 65g (2¹/₄oz) dried porcini mushrooms, soaked in hot water for 30 minutes
- 2 tbsp olive oil, plus extra for oiling a chopping board
- 2 garlic cloves, finely chopped
- 225g (8oz) girolle mushrooms
- 400g (14oz) Cheddar cheese, grated
- 65g (2¹/₄oz) Parmesan cheese, grated, plus extra to serve
- whole nutmeg, for grating
- 1 quantity Pasta dough (*see* page 296)
- '00' pasta flour, for dusting
- 1 quantity Sage butter (*see* page 298)
- salt and pepper

Serves 4–6 | Vegetarian

1 Heat the butter in a saucepan, add the onion and cook over a medium heat for 5 minutes, or until soft, stirring frequently. Drop in the marjoram and spinach, stir the mixture well to combine the flavours, and season with salt and pepper. Leave to cool.

2 Strain the porcini, reserving the liquid. Wipe them with a damp cloth and trim off any hard bits or debris. Heat the olive oil in a frying pan and fry the garlic gently, stirring, until it turns a very pale golden, then add the girolle mushrooms and cook over a high heat for 5 minutes, stirring frequently. Add the porcini, then turn down the heat to medium-low and cook for 15 minutes, adding a little of the reserved porcini liquid occasionally to make sure the mushrooms don't dry out. Season with salt and pepper. Leave to cool, then roughly chop. Put the spinach mixture in a bowl and grate in 6 or 7 strokes of nutmeg.

3 Using a pasta machine or a rolling pin roll out the pasta in 2 large strips. Position side by side on a clean tea towel to make a square, overlapping the edges that meet, brushing with water and pressing down gently to join. Use a fork to arrange the mushroom mixture 2cm (³/₄in) away from the edge of the pasta closest to you, keeping the mushroom strip about 4cm (1¹/₂in) wide. Cover the rest of the pasta sheet with the spinach mixture in a strip 8cm (3¹/₄in) wide and sprinkle with the cheeses. Starting with the mushroom edge, gently roll the pasta into a large cigar shape.

4 Wrap the roll tightly in a tea towel, then tie each end with kitchen string to hold the shape. Bring a large saucepan of salted water to the boil. Lower the rotolo into the water and simmer for 20 minutes. Use a metal skewer to pierce through the towel into the centre of the roll – if the skewer is hot to touch when removed, the rotolo is ready. Unwrap the rotolo, place it on a lightly oiled chopping board and cut into slices 2.5cm (1in) thick. Serve with Parmesan and the sage butter.

Rocket, watercress and chilli would give any cold a good spanking. If you don't have a cold, make the rocket soup anyway – it is delicious. Adding the leaves to the spinach soup base at the last minute or two keeps the colour really bright green. If you cook the spinach too long, it tends to look a little grey.

Spiced rocket soup with watercress oil

- 4 tbsp olive oil
- 3 shallots, finely chopped
- 1 tsp dried red chilli flakes
- 500g (1lb 2oz) potatoes, cut into 2cm (3/4in) cubes
- 2 litres (3 1/2 pints) hot Vegetable stock (*see* page 297)
- 750g (1lb 10oz) spinach
- 4 bunches of wild rocket, washed and patted dry
- 200ml (7fl oz) double cream
- salt and pepper

Watercress oil
- 1 bunch of watercress
- 250ml (9fl oz) olive oil
- salt and pepper

Serves 4–6 | Vegetarian

1   Heat the olive oil in a large saucepan, add the shallots and fry gently for 5 minutes, stirring frequently. Season lightly with salt and pepper, add the chilli flakes, then stir in the potatoes and cook for 3 minutes, stirring frequently. Add the hot stock and bring the soup to the boil, then reduce to a simmer and cook for 12–14 minutes until the potatoes are just tender. Remove from the heat.

2   Stir in the spinach and rocket and blend immediately in batches, until smooth, adding the cream while you blend; if you wait around before blending, you will begin to lose the electric green colour of the vegetables and some of their goodness too. Return the soup to the pan, check the seasoning and reheat gently ready for serving.

3   To make the watercress oil, wash and dry the watercress in a salad spinner. Transfer to a blender, pour in the olive oil and blend for 3–4 minutes for the maximum colour and flavour. Pour the oil through a very fine sieve or some muslin cloth. The oil will be a fantastic deep green colour. Serve the soup hot with a drizzle of the green watercress oil over the top and a rocket leaf or two.

Spinach soup with nutmeg

- 100ml (3 1/2fl oz) olive oil
- 2 white onions, chopped
- 2 garlic cloves
- 2 potatoes, cut into 2cm (3/4in) cubes
- 1 litre (1 3/4 pints) Vegetable stock (*see* page 297)
- 1.5kg (3lb 5oz) spinach
- 1/2 tsp freshly grated nutmeg
- juice of 1 lemon
- 50ml (2fl oz) double cream
- salt and pepper

Serves 4–6 | Vegetarian

1   Heat the olive oil in a saucepan, add the onions and cook over a medium heat for 5 minutes, until softened but not browned, stirring occasionally. Add the whole garlic cloves and cook for a further 4 minutes. Add the potatoes and stir well.

2   Pour in the stock, bring the soup to a simmer and cook for 15 minutes, or until the potatoes are tender. Add the spinach and cook for 2 minutes. Season with salt, pepper and nutmeg, then turn off the heat and leave to cool slightly. Transfer to a blender in batches and blend until smooth, adding a little of the cream and the lemon juice while you blend. Return the soup to the pan, check the seasoning, then reheat gently. Pour into bowls and garnish with dashes of the remaining cream.

Making a frittata big enough to share is great for two reasons. The first is that it looks amazing, and the second that it stays moist when bigger, and you can pack it full of flavour and goodness.

Sorrel frittata with mozzarella & Parmesan

- 50ml (2fl oz) olive oil
- 3 celery sticks, trimmed and cut into 2cm (3/4in) cubes
- 1 white onion, cut into 2cm (3/4in) cubes
- 1 garlic clove, chopped
- 500g (1lb 2oz) sorrel, tough stalks discarded
- 150g (5 1/2oz) pine nuts
- 6 large free-range eggs
- 1 ball mozzarella cheese
- 75g (2 3/4oz) Parmesan cheese, plus extra to serve
- salt and pepper
- chervil sprigs, to garnish

Serves 4–6 | Vegetarian

1   Heat the olive oil in a large frying pan, add the celery and onion and cook gently until the onion is translucent, stirring occasionally. Add the garlic and continue frying gently for 3 minutes. Add the sorrel and pine nuts to the pan, increase the heat, stirring and gently shaking the pan.

2   Break the eggs into a bowl and given them a good whisk, seasoning with salt and pepper. Pour the eggs into the pan, do not shake or stir, and reduce the heat to medium. Preheat the grill to high. As the eggs begin to set, use a spatula to loosen the frittata around the edge of the pan.

3   When the frittata is nearly cooked, after about 3 minutes, break up the mozzarella and scatter it over the top, then grate over the Parmesan. Put the pan under the grill (making sure you turn the handle away from the heat source) – this will cook the top of the frittata without having to turn it over, which can get messy. Grill for about 4 minutes, until the whole frittata is cooked, then give the pan a good shake to release the frittata from the base. Gently slide the frittata out onto a serving plate, then grate over a little extra Parmesan to serve and garnish with chervil sprigs.

The egg yolks make this soup so creamy and packed full of power. The sorrel cuts through the richness and leaves behind a lemony finish. Squeeze in extra lemon juice before serving for an extra lemony flavour.

Sorrel & egg yolk soup

- 75ml (2½fl oz) olive oil
- 6 celery sticks, trimmed and cut into 2cm (¾in) cubes
- 1 white onion, cut into 2cm (¾in) cubes
- 1 large potato, cut into 2cm (¾in) cubes
- 2 garlic cloves, chopped
- 100 ml (3½fl oz) medium-dry white wine
- 1 litre (1¾ pints) Vegetable stock (*see* page 297)
- 1 bunch sorrel, tough stalks discarded
- 2 tsp lemon juice
- 2 egg yolks
- salt and pepper

Serves 4–6 | Vegetarian

1   Heat the olive oil in a large saucepan, add the celery and onion and cook over a medium heat for 5 minutes, until softened but not browned, stirring occasionally. Add the potato and garlic, season with salt and pepper and cook for 15 minutes, stirring occasionally and without allowing the vegetables to catch on the base of the pan too much.

2   Add the wine and scrape up any browned bits in the bottom of the pan, then allow the liquid to evaporate before adding the stock. Bring to the boil, then reduce the heat and simmer for 20 minutes, until the potato is tender.

3   Gently tear the sorrel leaves, then add the lemon juice and sorrel to the pan and check the seasoning. Just before serving, with the pan still over the heat, add the egg yolks and mix vigorously with a balloon whisk. Pour the hot soup into bowls and serve.

Skill: Gratin

To gratinée a dish means to crisp up the top. A classic of the French kitchen, gratins often have a creamy sauce. They can all be finished off with breadcrumbs and heated under a hot grill for extra crunch. Artichokes have such a wonderful taste when cooked like this – use this first recipe to master the technique, then try the others overleaf.

Gratin of potato & artichokes with thyme & olive oil

- 2 large globe artichokes
- 1/2 lemon
- 750g (1lb 10oz) Linska or other medium-sized waxy potatoes, scrubbed
- 3 large shallots, finely chopped
- 4 garlic cloves, finely chopped
- 3 tbsp thyme leaves
- 75ml (2 1/2 fl oz) medium-dry white wine
- 1 litre (1 3/4 pints) Vegetable stock (*see* page 297)
- 200ml (7fl oz) double cream
- 100ml (3 1/2 fl oz) olive oil
- salt and pepper

Serves 4–6 | Vegetarian

1   Preheat the oven to 180°C/fan 160°C/gas mark 4. Peel off the tough outer leaves of the artichokes. Using a small, sharp knife, trim off the tops and the stalks, cutting each artichoke 5cm (2 in) up from the base to leave something the size of half an orange. Immerse the whole artichokes in cold salted water, otherwise the hairy choke will turn brown very quickly. Squeeze the 1/2 lemon over the bowl containing the artichokes. Cut the potatoes lengthways into slices 2cm (3/4in) thick, then scoop out the middle of each artichoke with a teaspoon and trim off any dark green parts left after pulling off the outer leaves.

2   Cut the artichokes in a similar way to the potatoes and place in a large mixing bowl with the shallots, garlic and thyme. Pour in the wine, vegetable stock and cream, drizzle in the olive oil and season. Mix well, using your hands, then arrange in a large, deep baking dish. Bake in the oven for 45 minutes, or until the potatoes are cooked and the cream mixture has reduced by half.

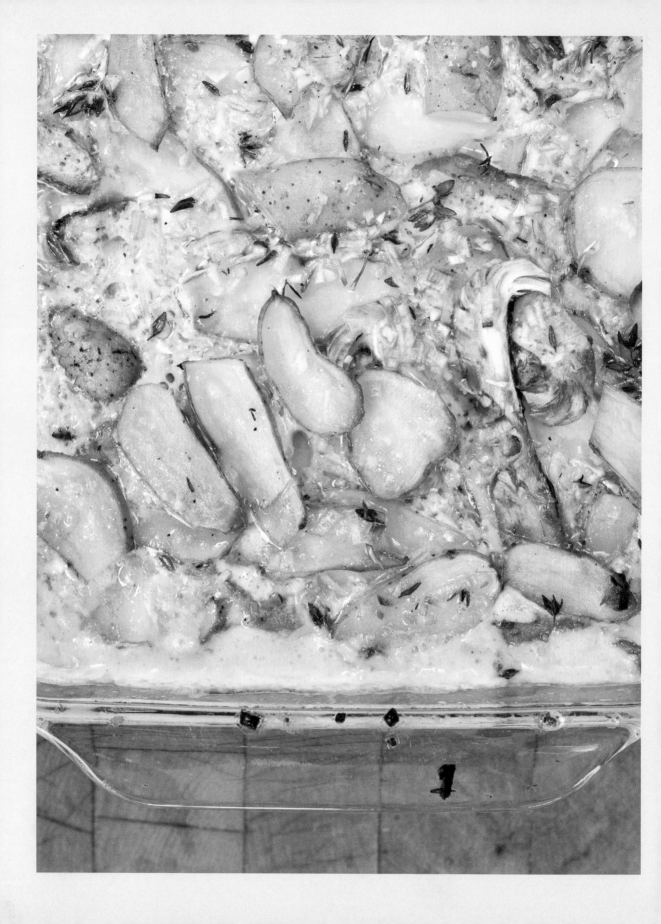

Gratin dauphinoise

- 1 garlic clove
- 2kg (4lb 8oz) floury potatoes
- 500ml (18fl oz) milk
- 500ml (18fl oz) double cream
- 2 thyme sprigs
- 1 tsp freshly grated nutmeg
- salt and pepper

Serves 4–6 | Vegetarian

1 Preheat the oven to 160°C/fan 140°C/gas mark 3. Rub the inside of a gratin dish with the garlic clove – you will use at least half the clove just by rubbing vigorously. This adds a very subtle aroma of garlic rather than the aggressive finish that results from putting the whole clove into the potato mixture.

2 Put the potatoes into a large mixing bowl. Gently heat the milk and cream together with the thyme sprigs without boiling to infuse the liquid with the thyme flavour. Pour half the warm liquid over the sliced potatoes and mix well with your hands, making sure that every slice is covered.

3 Using a slotted spoon, arrange the potato slices in the gratin dish in overlapping layers, seasoning with a touch of salt, pepper and nutmeg as you go, and making sure not to leave any gaps. Pour the remaining liquid over the potatoes and bake for 1 hour 20 minutes, or until the potatoes are cooked and the top is golden brown. Don't cook for too long or the fats will separate, resulting in an oily finish.

Turnip & celeriac gratin

- 1 garlic clove
- 1kg (2lb 4oz) celeriac
- 1kg (2lb 4oz) turnips
- 500ml (18fl oz) milk
- 500ml (18fl oz) double cream
- 2 lemon thyme sprigs
- 1 tsp freshly grated nutmeg
- salt and pepper

Serves 4–6 | Vegetarian

1 Follow the method above, preparing the celeriac and turnips in the same way as the potatoes and using the lemon thyme in place of the ordinary thyme.

Pumpkin gratin

- 1.5kg (3lb 5oz) Crown Prince, or other firm pumpkin
- 2 garlic cloves, finely chopped
- 3 tbsp thyme leaves
- 3 tbsp olive oil
- 500ml (18fl oz) double cream
- 250ml (9fl oz) medium-dry white wine
- 250ml (9fl oz) Vegetable stock (see page 297)
- 250g (9oz) Cheddar cheese, grated
- salt and pepper

Serves 4–6 | Vegetarian

1 Preheat the oven to 180°C/fan 160°C/gas mark 4. Peel the pumpkin, then cut in half and scoop out and reserve the seeds. Slice the flesh into strips 1cm (½in) thick and put them into a large mixing bowl. Heat a dry frying pan over a medium-high heat, add the reserved pumpkin seeds and then shake the pan until they start to crackle and toast. Add three-quarters of the toasted seeds, the garlic, thyme leaves and olive oil to the pumpkin in the bowl, season with salt and pepper and mix well by hand.

2 Lay the pumpkin strips in a gratin dish in overlapping layers. Mix the cream and wine into the stock, then pour the liquid into the corner of the dish, trying not to dislodge the strips too much. Sprinkle over the Cheddar and then the rest of the toasted pumpkin seeds. Bake for 1 hour 20 minutes, making sure that the cheese doesn't colour too much – if it starts to darken, turn down the heat slightly and cover the dish with a piece of foil.

Radicchio Trevisano & bacon gratin

- 2 heads of radicchio Trevisano, outer leaves discarded and leaves separated
- 750g (1lb 10oz) Linska or other medium-sized waxy potatoes, scrubbed and cut into discs 2cm (¾in) wide
- 12 streaky bacon rashers, cut into strips 2cm (¾in) wide
- 4 garlic cloves, finely chopped
- 4 shallots, finely chopped
- 3 tbsp roughly chopped oregano
- 300ml (½ pint) medium-dry white wine
- 300ml (½ pint) double cream
- 250ml (9fl oz) Vegetable stock (see page 297)
- 3 tbsp olive oil
- salt and pepper

Serves 4–6

1 Preheat the oven to 180°C/fan 160°C/gas mark 4. Chop the radicchio and place in a large bowl with the potatoes. Add the bacon, garlic, shallots and oregano, season with salt and pepper and mix well. Pour in the wine, cream, stock and oil, mix again, then arrange in a gratin dish and bake for 1 hour, or until the potatoes are cooked.

Golden beetroot gratin

- 1.25kg (2lb 12oz) golden beetroot, sliced into discs 1cm (½in) thick
- 250g (9oz) fresh horseradish root, peeled and finely grated
- 2 garlic cloves, finely chopped
- 3 tbsp thyme leaves
- 3 tbsp olive oil
- 500ml (18fl oz) double cream
- 250ml (9fl oz) medium-dry white wine
- 250ml (9fl oz) Vegetable stock (see page 297)
- 250g (9oz) Gruyère cheese, grated
- salt and pepper

Serves 4–6 | Vegetarian

1 Follow the method for Pumpkin gratin (left).

Leek, spring onion & potato gratin

- 750g (1lb 10oz) leeks
- 1kg (2lb 4oz) Roosevelt or other waxy potatoes, scrubbed
- 1 bunch of spring onions, trimmed and finely chopped
- 1 garlic clove, finely chopped
- 2 tbsp roughly chopped flat leaf parsley
- 2 tbsp thyme leaves
- 100ml (3½fl oz) olive oil
- 200ml (3½fl oz) double cream
- 75ml (3½fl oz) medium-dry white wine
- salt and pepper

Serves 4–6 | Vegetarian

1 Preheat the oven to 180°C/fan 160°C/gas mark 4. Remove and discard the outer layers of the leeks and cut off the dark green tops. Cut the leeks lengthways in half 1cm (½in) up from the base, then wash them under cold running water to remove any sand or soil. Cut the potatoes lengthways into 2cm (¾in) thick slices and the leeks similarly, then put them into a large mixing bowl and mix well. Add the spring onions, garlic and parsley, season with salt and pepper and throw in the thyme leaves. Pour in the wine and cream and olive oil and bake for 1 hour 20 minutes, or until the potatoes are cooked and the top is golden brown.

Radicchio is an interesting leaf. In its raw state it lends itself brilliantly to salads, adding a bitter undertone to a dish, but when cooked, it's transformed into a gutsy vegetable that actually tastes a little sweet.

Chargrilled radicchio

- 2 heads of radicchio, damaged outer leaves discarded
- 4 tbsp marjoram leaves
- 4 tbsp balsamic vinegar
- 4 tbsp olive oil
- salt and pepper

Serves 4–6 | Vegetarian

1 Using a large, sharp knife, cut the radicchio heads lengthways into quarters and then eighths, and finally sixteenths, retaining a part of the core and stalk in each piece to prevent the leaves falling apart.

2 Prepare a charcoal barbecue (*see* step 2, page 228) or heat a griddle pan until very hot. Arrange the radicchio pieces on the barbecue rack, or griddle, and cook for 6 minutes until they are golden brown and lightly charred in some places. Turn over and cook the other side in the same way.

3 Put the radicchio on a serving dish. Scatter the marjoram leaves over it, then drizzle over the balsamic vinegar, followed by the olive oil. Season lightly and serve.

The sweetness of the pancetta and wine help to balance the bitterness of the chicory. If you can't get Gewürztraminer, use a medium to sweet white wine instead.

Roasted chicory with pancetta & Gewürztraminer

- **6 heads of red or white chicory, damaged outer leaves discarded**
- **10 garlic cloves, thinly sliced**
- **24 slices of pancetta**
- **200ml (7fl oz) Gewürztraminer wine**
- **150ml (¼ pint) olive oil**
- **salt and pepper**

Serves 4–6

1   Preheat the oven to 190°C/fan 170°C/gas mark 5. Cut the chicory lengthways into quarters (they will look like gondolas). Hold a quarter in one hand and use your other hand to insert 2 or 3 slices of garlic into the gaps between the leaves, pushing them in snugly. Take a strip of pancetta and wrap it diagonally round the chicory leaves. Repeat with the remaining chicory quarters.

2   Place your 'gondolas' on a roasting tray covered with baking parchment. Drizzle with the wine and olive oil, and season with salt and pepper. Roast for 20 minutes, or until the pancetta is crispy and the wine has evaporated into the chicory.

You can always substitute soured cream for the double cream in this dish, or omit it completely for a lighter dish.

Creamed white chicory with leeks & celery

- 100g (3½oz) butter
- 400g (14oz) celery heart, very thinly sliced
- 2 shallots, very thinly sliced
- 1 garlic clove, very thinly sliced
- 750g (1lb 10oz) white chicory, very thinly sliced
- 750g (1lb 10oz) leeks, white parts only, very thinly sliced
- 250ml (9fl oz) medium-dry white wine
- 100ml (3½fl oz) double cream
- salt and pepper

Serves 4–6 | Vegetarian

1   Heat the butter in a saucepan, add the celery, shallots and garlic and cook gently for 10 minutes, stirring frequently. Add the chicory and leeks, season with salt and pepper and continue to cook for 5 minutes, stirring all the while to get a good coating of butter all over the vegetables. Add the wine, increase the heat and allow the liquid to evaporate, then add the cream.

2   Reduce the heat to low and let the cream heat up, but not boil – over-reduction of the cream makes for a very heavy dish, and we want to keep this light. Check the seasoning and serve hot.

Creamed lettuce

If you are not keen on the bitter flavour of chicory, even though most of the bitterness is cooked away, you can use Baby Gem lettuce instead. Prepare and cook as above, adding a little celery salt to the lettuce before serving.

I always chuckle to myself when I cook this dish. Ahh, the old prawn cocktail years, eh? But if you get this right, it is a wicked dish and one definitely worth keeping in your repertoire. I've included a vegetarian version too, but if you wanted to combine the prawns with the salsify, it just gets even better.

Chicory & prawn cocktail boats

- **750g (1lb 10oz) large cooked and peeled prawns**
- **3 tbsp Homemade mayonnaise (*see* page 297)**
- **3 tbsp Classic tomato sauce (*see* page 211)**
- **3 heads of white chicory, outer leaves separated**
- **juice of 1 lemon**
- **3 tbsp finely diced tomato**
- **2 tbsp finely chopped chives**
- **salt and pepper**
- **chervil sprigs, to garnish**

Serves 4–6

1   Lightly wash the prawns and leave them to dry in a colander.

2   Put the mayonnaise and tomato sauce into a large bowl and mix together. Cut the chicory hearts in half and then into very thin half-moons. Add to the dressing in the bowl. Now add the prawns, lemon juice, diced tomato and half the chives. Mix well and check the seasoning.

3   Arrange the reserved chicory leaves on a large serving plate and place a tablespoonful of the prawn mixture at the base of each leaf. Garnish with chervil sprigs and serve immediately.

Chicory & salsify cocktail boats

For a vegetarian version of the above, replace the prawns with 6 large salsify, peeled, chopped into prawn-sized pieces and blanched for 6–8 minutes in a saucepan of salted water.

Kale is one of the superfoods, which means that these dishes are super-packed with goodness and flavour. Both work brilliantly with spinach too. Keep going on the pepper for a real kick, and serve with boiled potatoes and carrots.

Braised curly kale with garlic & soy sauce

- 500g (1lb 2oz) green curly kale
- 3 tbsp virgin olive oil
- 1 tsp chopped fresh red chilli
- 1 garlic clove, chopped
- 2 tsp light soy sauce
- salt and pepper

Serves 4–6 | Vegetarian

1   Remove any yellowing bits or tough stalks from the kale, then reserve the leaves in cold water. Bring a large saucepan of water to the boil and season with salt. Drain the kale, add to the pan and cook for 6 minutes. Drain again and keep warm.

2   Heat the olive oil in a frying pan, add the chilli and garlic and fry gently for about 3 minutes, until the garlic begins to colour. Immediately put the cooked kale into the pan and stir well. Season lightly with pepper and the soy sauce, and cook for 4 minutes, stirring frequently. Serve warm.

Creamed purple kale with pepper & lemon

- 750g (1lb 10oz) purple kale
- 3 tbsp virgin olive oil
- 3 shallots, finely diced
- 200ml (7fl oz) medium-dry white wine
- 250ml (9fl oz) double cream
- juice of 1 lemon
- salt and white pepper

Serves 4–6 | Vegetarian

1   Remove any yellowing bits or tough stalks from the kale, then reserve the leaves in cold water. Bring a large saucepan of water to the boil and season with salt. Drain the kale, add to the pan and cook for 6 minutes. Drain again and keep warm.

2   Heat the olive oil in a frying pan, add the shallots and fry gently for 4–5 minutes, until they begin to colour. Pour in the wine and allow it to evaporate before adding the cream. Just as the cream starts to bubble, add the cooked kale and squeeze in the lemon juice. Grind in some white pepper and season lightly with salt. Allow the liquid to reduce slightly, then serve.

Try to cut the vegetables really thinly for this salad: the finer they are, the more delicate the salad will be. Marinating in the fridge with lemon juice will make the cabbage just a little tender, which improves the texture.

White cabbage salad with raisins & cranberries

- 1 small white cabbage
- 250g (9oz) carrots
- 1 bunch of spring onions, trimmed
- 2 tbsp Homemade mayonnaise (*see* page 297)
- 2 tbsp salad cream
- 2 tbsp Greek yogurt
- juice of 1 lemon
- 150g (5¹/₂oz) dried cranberries
- 150g (5¹/₂oz) raisins
- salt and pepper

Serves 4–6 | Vegetarian

1   Shred the cabbage, carrots and spring onions.

2   Put the mayonnaise, salad cream and yogurt into a large mixing bowl. Squeeze in the lemon juice, mix together and season with salt and pepper. Add the cranberries and raisins, mix well, then add the shredded vegetables. Stir thoroughly, cover with clingfilm and leave to rest in the refrigerator for 1 hour before serving.

Caraway adds a magic quality to this dish. Some people don't use caraway at all in their cooking, but I think it adds an amazing flavour to cabbage and rice dishes.

Peppered Savoy cabbage with caraway & lemon

- 1 small Savoy cabbage
- 2 tsp caraway seeds
- 150g (5¹/₂oz) butter
- juice and finely grated rind of
  1 unwaxed lemon
- salt and pepper

Serves 4–6 | Vegetarian

1   Discard the outer leaves from the cabbage, keeping 3 or 4 whole large leaves to line the steamer. Wash the outer leaves in cold water and drain, then cut the cabbage into quarters and cut out the core. Slice the quarters into fine matchsticks and put them into the bamboo steamer lined with cabbage leaves. (Alternatively use a metal colander or steamer with lid, that fits over a saucepan). Sprinkle over the caraway seeds and lightly season with salt and pepper. Place half the butter on top of the cabbage and then fold the leaves over the top. Cover with a lid and steam the cabbage for 25 minutes.

2   Transfer the cabbage to a serving bowl, add the rest of the butter, lemon rind and juice and lightly season again. Serve straight away.

This is a real one-pot wonder, with big flavours and hearty textures, perfect for winter. Use white wine if you can't find cider, but if you are lucky enough to find locally made cider, it will make all the difference.

Braised Savoy cabbage with apples, cider & cinnamon

- 1 small Savoy cabbage
- 75g (2³/₄oz) butter
- 1 white onion, thinly sliced
- 1 cinnamon stick
- 2 bay leaves
- 75ml (2¹/₂fl oz) olive oil
- 150g (5¹/₂oz) sultanas
- 1 large Bramley apple, peeled, cored and thinly sliced
- 250ml (9fl oz) cider
- salt and pepper

Serves 4–6 | Vegetarian

1   Discard the outer leaves from the cabbage, then shred the remainder as finely as you can.

2   Melt the butter in a large saucepan, add the onion, cinnamon, bay leaves and olive oil and cook over a medium heat for 5–6 minutes, stirring frequently, until the onion is melted and soft. Add the cabbage, sultanas and apple, and cook for 35 minutes until the cabbage has wilted completely, stirring frequently.

3   Add the cider and season with salt and pepper, stir one last time, then cover the pan and reduce the heat to its lowest setting. Cook for 1 hour, checking every 15 minutes that the cabbage is not sticking. When ready, the cabbage should be soft but not falling apart, and taste slightly sweet and not too wet. I like my cabbage nice and peppery, but adjust the seasoning to your taste and you are ready to serve.

This is one of the first dishes I ever prepared in the Roux brothers' kitchens. We used to make so much that it would take me nearly half the day just to cut up the cabbages. The version below is a play on 25 years of experimenting. It's good with baked potatoes or some roasted duck.

Red cabbage stew with red wine, pears & brown sugar

- 1 small red cabbage
- 75g (2³⁄₄oz) butter
- 50ml (2fl oz) olive oil
- 2 red onions, thinly sliced
- 1 garlic clove, thinly sliced
- 1 cinnamon stick
- 2 bay leaves
- 1 tsp juniper berries
- 1 Comice pear, peeled, cored and cut into 4cm (1¹⁄₂in) pieces
- 1 Bramley apple, peeled, cored and cut into 4cm (1¹⁄₂in) pieces
- 150g (5¹⁄₂oz) raisins
- 100ml (3¹⁄₂fl oz) red wine vinegar
- 100g (3¹⁄₂oz) soft light brown sugar
- salt and pepper

Serves 4–6 | Vegetarian

1 Preheat the oven to 150°C/fan 140°C/gas mark 2. Discard the outer leaves from the cabbage, then cut the head into quarters. Cut out the core, then slice the quarters as thinly as you can.

2 Melt the butter with the olive oil in a flameproof casserole dish, add the red onion and garlic and cook over a medium heat for 6–8 minutes, stirring frequently, until the onion is melted and soft. Add the cinnamon, bay leaves, juniper berries and some salt and pepper and cook for 5 minutes to get the flavours going, stirring occasionally. Add the red cabbage and stir well, then the pear and apple and stir again. Add the raisins, vinegar and sugar, then increase the heat and get the ingredients sweating and giving off their aromas.

3 Cover the casserole dish and transfer to the oven for 2 hours, stirring every 15 minutes. Check the seasoning and serve hot.

I put different types of brassica into this gratin, partnering some with Stilton and the other with Cheddar. You can see the difference between them by how they colour, but they both have the best golden crust. This just has to be one of my favourite dishes in this book.

Cauliflower & broccoli cheese au gratin

- 1 cauliflower
- 1 head of Romanesco broccoli
- 1 head of regular broccoli
- 100g (3¹/₂oz) Stilton cheese, crumbled
- 50g (1³/₄oz) Cheddar cheese, grated
- 50g (1³/₄oz) Parmesan cheese, freshly grated

Cheesy béchamel sauce
- 50g (2oz) butter
- 50g (2oz) plain flour
- 450ml (16fl oz) milk
- whole nutmeg, for grating
- 150g (5¹/₂oz) Cheddar cheese, grated
- 50g (1³/₄oz) Parmesan cheese, freshly grated
- salt and pepper

Serves 4–6 | Vegetarian

1   First make the sauce. Melt the butter in a saucepan until it foams. Mix in the flour and cook over a low heat, stirring, for 4–5 minutes without allowing the roux to colour. With the pan still on the heat, slowly whisk in half the milk, then increase the heat, bring to the boil and cook until thickened, whisking well to avoid lumps. Season lightly with salt but quite generously with pepper and nutmeg, then add the Cheddar and the Parmesan. Keep the sauce warm while you prepare the vegetables.

2   Cut the cauliflower and the broccolis into florets. Drop the florets into a large saucepan of salted boiling water and cook for 6–8 minutes, or until the florets are tender but still firm to the bite. Preheat the grill to medium. Drain the florets in a colander and allow the steam to rise everything to dry off, which stops the dish becoming waterlogged.

3   Arrange the cauliflower on one side of an ovenproof dish and the broccoli florets on the other. Pour the warm cheese sauce evenly over them and sprinkle the rest of the Cheddar and Parmesan over the dish. Scatter the Stilton over the broccoli side of the dish and place under the grill for 12–15 minutes until the topping turns a deep golden colour. Serve straight from the dish.

I cooked this dish for my kids the day before the photos for this book were taken. They loved it, and I've included it to show how good simple cooking will get your children coming back for more.

Crunchy broccoli salad with toasted almonds & hazelnut oil

- 750g (1lb 10oz) broccoli florets
- 200g (7oz) flaked almonds
- 1 large beef tomato, cut into 2cm (3/4in) cubes
- 100ml (3½fl oz) hazelnut or olive oil
- 50ml (2fl oz) cider vinegar
- salt and pepper

Serves 4–6 | Vegetarian

1   Drop the broccoli florets into a large saucepan of salted boiling water and blanch for 3 minutes.

2   Meanwhile, heat a dry frying pan over a medium-high heat, tip in the flaked almonds and shake the pan until they start to toast – make sure you don't colour them too much. Remove from the heat and tip on to a plate.

3   Drain the broccoli well and put it into a large bowl. Add the tomato, then drizzle in the oil and vinegar and season with salt and pepper. Toss gently to mix all the flavours together, then turn on to a serving plate.

I eat a lot of Asian-influenced food, and this dish is my take on a Chinese stir-fry. I love rice wine vinegar – it is a great way to lift flavours and works beautifully with broccoli and bean sprouts.

Stir-fried sprouts & broccoli

- 75ml (2¹/₂fl oz) sesame oil
- 3 tbsp fresh root ginger, cut into fine matchsticks
- 1 garlic clove, thinly sliced
- 1 tsp dried red chilli flakes
- 400g (14oz) bean sprouts
- 750g (1lb 10oz) broccoli florets, cut into quarters
- 2 tsp caster sugar
- 50ml (2fl oz) rice wine vinegar
- 50ml (2fl oz) light soy sauce

Serves 4–6 | Vegetarian

1   Heat the sesame oil in a large frying pan and, just before it begins to smoke, add the ginger, garlic and chilli flakes and cook over a high heat for 30 seconds.

2   Add the bean sprouts and stir-fry for 30 seconds, then add the broccoli and stir-fry for 2–3 minutes. Sprinkle in the sugar and add the vinegar and soy sauce. Serve immediately.

The knowledge of pickling is something that every household should have and comes into its own when there is a glut of fresh produce to preserve. Don't be deterred by the time it takes – there is a magic in waiting for a pickle to mature and increase in flavour. Giving a gift of a pickle to your mates is a great way to show off your skills. In fact, why not set up a pickles club and pickle (and swap) once a month?

Pickled cabbage with caraway & mustard

– 1 white cabbage
– 60g (2¼oz) sea salt
– 1.5 litres (2¾pints) pickling malt vinegar
– 600ml (1 pint) white pickling vinegar
– 10 white peppercorns
– 1 tbsp caraway seeds
– 1 tbsp yellow mustard seeds
– 1 cinnamon stick

Makes 1 large (1.5 litre) jar
Vegetarian

1   Discard the outer leaves from the cabbage, then shred the rest as finely as you can. Lay the shredded cabbage in layers in a large colander set over a pan, sprinkling each layer with the salt. Cover with clingfilm and leave to stand in a cool place for 24 hours. Drain the cabbage, rinse thoroughly under cold running water and drain again.

2   Put the remaining ingredients in a saucepan and bring to the boil. Remove from the heat and leave to marinate for 3 hours.

3   Sterilize a large Kilner-type glass jar by putting the jar and lid into a large saucepan of boiling water for 5 minutes. Remove and leave to dry.

4   Pack the cabbage into the sterilized glass jar ¾ full, removing any remaining water by turning upside down. Pour in the vinegar and spices. Seal the lid of the jar closed and turn upside down, to ensure the vinegar is well distributed. Store in a cool, dark place for 2 weeks before using. It will keep, unopened, for up to 2 months in cool, dark conditions. Once opened, refrigerate and use within 2 weeks.

Pickled Jerusalem artichokes

- 500g (1lb 2oz) Jerusalem artichokes
- 600ml (1 pint) white pickling vinegar
- rind of 1 unwaxed lemon, cut in fine strips
- 2 bay leaves
- sea salt

Makes 1 large (1.5 litre) jar | Vegetarian

1   Cook the artichokes in a large saucepan of salted boiling water for 6–8 minutes until just tender. Drain, leave to cool completely and then chill in the refrigerator.

2   Meanwhile, bring the vinegar, lemon rind, bay leaves and 2 tablespoons salt to the boil and continue to boil for 10 minutes. Strain, discarding the zest and bay leaves. Leave to cool completely and then put into the refrigerator to chill.

3   Sterilize a Kilner-type jar (follow step 3 of the method on page 180), then fill and store as described in step 4.

Cauliflower chutney piccalilli style

- 2.5 litres (4½ pints) water
- 250g (9oz) sea salt
- 250g (9oz) French beans, topped and tailed and cut into 2cm (¾in) lengths
- 200g (7oz) peeled and deseeded marrow, cut into 2cm (¾in) cubes
- 1 small cucumber, topped and tailed, deseeded and cut into 2cm (¾in) pieces
- 1 cauliflower, cut into small florets
- 200g (7oz) baby (pickling) onions
- 750ml (1¼ pints) cider vinegar
- 150g (5½oz) soft light brown sugar
- 1 garlic clove
- 6cm (2½in) piece of fresh root ginger, peeled and finely diced
- ½tsp Chinese five-spice powder
- ½tsp freshly grated nutmeg
- ½tsp turmeric
- ½tsp English mustard powder
- ½tsp paprika
- 2–3 tbsp plain flour

Makes 1 large (1.5 litre) jar | Vegetarian

1   Bring the water to the boil in a large saucepan, add the salt and stir. Divide the water between 2 large bowls. Put the French beans, marrow and cucumber in one bowl and the cauliflower and the baby onions in the other. Use a saucepan lid or small plate to push the vegetables in the water. Cover each bowl with clingfilm and leave in a cool place for 24 hours. Drain the vegetables, rinse under cold running water and drain again. Return to the separate cleaned and dried bowls.

2   Heat the vinegar and sugar in a saucepan. Smash the garlic clove with the back of a heavy knife, drop it in the hot vinegar along with the ginger and bring to the boil. Add the cauliflower and baby onions, five-spice powder and nutmeg and cook for 4–5 minutes. Add the rest of the vegetables and cook for 5 minutes more – keep the vegetables al dente. Lift out of the liquid with a slotted spoon to a bowl, reserving the vinegar.

3   To make the piccalilli sauce that coats all the vegetables, mix the turmeric, mustard and paprika together in a small bowl, add the flour and then spoon in some of the warm vinegar. Work to a smooth paste, then add the paste to the remaining warm vinegar and cook over a low heat for about 15 minutes, until the sauce has thickened and the floury taste has been cooked out. Keep stirring so the sauce doesn't stick. Pour the sauce on the cooling vegetables and mix well. Leave to cool.

4   Sterilize a Kilner-type jar (follow step 3 of the method on page 180, then fill and store as described in step 4 (though no need to drain off any water).

Pickled ramps

- 200g (7oz) ramps (wild garlic bulbs)
- 125ml (4fl oz) cider vinegar
- 1 tsp caraway seeds
- 1 tsp yellow mustard seeds
- 1 cinnamon stick
- 3 tbsp soft light brown sugar

Makes 1 medium (1 litre) jar | Vegetarian

1   Trim the ramps, then wash them well and drain. Bring the vinegar to the boil in a saucepan and add the caraway and mustard seeds, cinnamon stick and sugar. Boil for 5 minutes.

2   Sterilize a Kilner-type jar (follow step 3 of the method on page 180), then fill and store as described in step 4.

Pickled young cucumbers

- 30 small young cucumbers
- 2 fresh large green chillies, roughly chopped
- 1 garlic bulb, cloves separated, peeled and crushed
- 6 bay leaves
- 25g (1oz) allspice berries
- 150ml (¼ pint) white pickling vinegar
- 1.5 litres (2¾ pints) warm water
- 1 tsp black peppercorns
- 2½ tbsp sea salt

Makes 1 large (1.5 litre) jar | Vegetarian

1   Sterilize a Kilner-type jar (follow step 3 of the method on page 180), then pack in a third of the cucumbers. Add half the chilli, a third of the garlic and a couple of bay leaves. Repeat the layering twice more, but using the allspice berries in place of the chilli for the final layer. Add the vinegar to the warm water and peppercorns in a bowl and stir in the sea salt until dissolved. Pour the mixture into the jar, then leave to cool completely. Seal the jar and store in a sunlit place. The cucumbers will turn an electric green colour within a week and will keep, unopened, up to 2 months in a cool, dark place. Once opened, refrigerate and use within 2 weeks.

Pickled radishes

- 500g (1lb 2oz) radishes, topped and tailed
- 4 garlic cloves
- 600ml (1 pint) white pickling vinegar
- 2 bay leaves
- sea salt

Makes 1 medium (1 litre) jar | Vegetarian

1   Cook the radishes with the garlic cloves in a large saucepan of salted boiling water for 5 minutes, until just tender. Drain, leave to cool completely, then chill in the refrigerator.

2   Meanwhile, bring the vinegar, bay leaves and 2 tablespoons sea salt to the boil in a saucepan and boil for 10 minutes. Strain, discarding the bay leaves, leave to cool, then chill in the refrigerator.

3   Sterilize a Kilner-type jar (follow step 3 of the method on page 180), then fill and store as described in step 4 (though no need to drain off any water).

Spiced beetroot à la gourmet

- 8 red beetroots
- 1 quantity House dressing (see page 297)
- 2–3 cloves
- 1 tsp celery seeds
- 1 garlic clove, lightly crushed
- 2 bay leaves
- 1 dried small red chilli
- salt and pepper

Serves 4–6 | Vegetarian

1   Preheat the oven to 180°C/fan 160°C/gas mark 4. Put the beetroot on a roasting tray and roast for about 1 hour for medium-sized beetroot, or until cooked but not soft. Leave until cool.

2   Rub off and peel away the skins of the beetroot, then trim off the remaining tops and tails. Slice them through the round into thin discs. Put the sliced beets into a bowl, cover with a plate and leave to cool completely.

3   Pour off any juice that has accumulated in the beetroot bowl into a separate bowl and then put the beetroot into the refrigerator to chill. Mix the dressing, cloves, celery seeds, garlic, bay leaves and chilli into the beetroot juice. Season with salt and pepper, cover with clingfilm and leave to marinate in a cool place overnight. To serve, strain the spiced dressing through a fine sieve over the chilled

I remember as a young child my mother taking me to a restaurant and ordering this dish. I couldn't believe it when this huge vegetable from another world arrived at the table, and I was even more transfixed watching my mum eat. Now my kids watch me do the same thing. The further you work into the artichoke removing the petals, the more flesh there will be to eat at the base. Don't forget a finger bowl...

Whole artichoke with lemon butter dip

– **4 large globe artichokes**
– **200g (7oz) butter**
– **juice of 1 lemon**
– **4 tbsp finely chopped chives**
– **salt and pepper**
– **lemon cheeks, to serve (*see* page 44)**

Serves 4 | Vegetarian

1   Using a small, sharp knife, trim off the top 5cm (2in) of each artichoke and the whole stalk. Put the artichokes into a large saucepan of salted boiling water and cook for 12–15 minutes, depending on their size, until cooked. To check if they are ready, insert the tip of a small knife into the base where the stalk used to be – you are looking for a slight resistance but not firmness.

2   When the artichokes are nearly cooked, set a heatproof bowl over the pan and melt the butter in it. Whisk in the lemon juice and season with salt and pepper. Remove the bowl from the pan and add the chives.

3   To serve, drain the artichokes and stand each one flat on its base. Spoon over some of the butter mixture, then put the rest of it into ramekins, one for each artichoke. Get your guests to pull off each petal of the artichoke, dip the fleshy base into the butter mixture and scrape the flesh off with their teeth. Serve with lemon cheeks for squeezing over.

This is one of those recipes that is truly satisfying to complete. It not only delivers a sense of achievement, but tastes fantastic too. You would never be able to buy these artichokes in a delicatessen, so when you put them on the table in front of your guests, they'll be blown away.

Wine-braised artichokes stuffed with herbs

– **1 bunch flat leaf parsley**
– **1/2 lemon**
– **12 small globe artichokes**
– **2 tbsp finely chopped mint**
– **2 tbsp finely chopped basil**
– **3 garlic cloves, finely chopped**
– **150ml (1/4 pint) olive oil**
– **200ml (7oz) medium-dry white wine**
– **salt and pepper**

Serves 4–6 | Vegetarian

1   Pick the parsley leaves from their stalks and put the stalks into a pan of cold water with the lemon. Using a small, sharp knife, trim the artichoke stalks down to 4cm (1¹/₂in). Peel off the tough outer leaves, leaving only the pale tender centres. Trim off the tops and scoop out the central chokes – there isn't much of this in small artichokes, but you need to create a cavity for the stuffing. Put the prepared artichokes into the bowl with the water, lemon and parsley stalks.

2   For the stuffing, mix the parsley leaves and other herbs and garlic together and season well with salt and pepper. Drain the artichokes, then press the mixture into the cavity of each artichoke.

3   Pour the olive oil into a heavy-based saucepan large enough to contain all the artichokes but small enough for them to fit snugly. Place the artichokes, stuffed side down, in the pan. Throw any leftover herb mixture over the top. Pour in the wine and add enough water to come a third of the way up the sides of the artichokes and bring to the boil. Reduce the heat, cover with a sheet of baking parchment and put the lid on top. Cook gently for about 30 minutes until the water has evaporated and the artichokes have begun to brown at the base – the caramelization is important to this dish, so try to make sure you get some colour on the artichokes. Serve hot.

I once cooked this dish for 100 people while I was working in the galley of a yacht sailing around Manhattan Island. It was one of the most difficult kitchens I have ever worked in, but the memory of serving up this amazing-looking dish and the guests' reactions made it worthwhile.

Artichokes with spinach, poached egg & smoked salmon

- 4 globe artichokes, trimmed and stalks removed (*see* step 1, page 184)
- 25g (1oz) butter
- 50ml (2fl oz) olive oil
- 800g (1lb 12oz) spinach, stalks removed
- 50ml (2fl oz) white wine vinegar
- 4 large free-range eggs, at room temperature
- 4 slices of smoked salmon
- sea salt and pepper

Serves 4

1 Put the artichokes into a large saucepan of salted boiling water and cook for 13–15 minutes, depending on their size, until tender – there should be the faintest resistance when you pierce the base with a small, sharp knife.

2 Melt the butter with the olive oil in a large saucepan, add the spinach and sauté over a high heat for 5 minutes, stirring frequently. Season with salt and pepper and keep warm.

3 Add the vinegar to a saucepan of salted boiling water. Crack an egg into a cup, pour it into the water and watch it sink quickly to the bottom but immediately form a white protective covering around the yolk – the salt and vinegar help to set the egg white. Lift the poached egg out with a slotted spoon when cooked to your liking: 3 minutes for a runny yolk, 5 minutes for fairly firm. Keep warm while you cook the rest of the eggs in the same way.

4 Place each artichoke on a serving plate and fill with a quarter of the spinach. Sit a warm poached egg on each, top with a slice of smoked salmon, grind over plenty of pepper and sprinkle with salt flakes.

I once prepared so many artichokes in one year that I nearly decided to change my name to 'Arthachoke'. Choose young, purple-tipped globe artichokes, which you can find in lots of places now – the best will be from your local market.

Marinated artichokes with lemon & marjoram

- 12 small violet globe artichokes, stalks attached
- finely grated rind and juice of 1 unwaxed lemon, plus lemon slices from 1/4 lemon
- 75ml (18fl oz) virgin olive oil
- 1 sprig of marjoram, chopped
- salt and pepper

Serves 4–6 | Vegetarian

1   Bring a large saucepan of water to the boil and drop in the whole artichokes. They will float, so use a heatproof plate or small pan lid to keep them under the hot water, otherwise they will be half-cooked. Cook for about 12 minutes, then remove one artichoke and pierce with a small, sharp knife at the base of the stem: there should be a firm but smooth feeling to the knife going in. If there is any resistance, cook for a few more minutes.

2   When the artichokes are ready, drain and refresh them under cold running water. Leave in cold water for 1 minute, then peel off the outer layer of leaves of each artichoke in turn until you reach the sweet flesh inside. Lay the prepared artichokes on a chopping board and peel off and discard the outer layer of each stalk. Cut off the top of each artichoke about 6cm (2 1/2 in) down from the tip. Using a teaspoon, spoon out any choke sitting in the exposed heart – there tends not to be any choke with these young artichokes, but it is worth checking. Cut the artichokes in half.

3   Put the prepared artichokes into a mixing bowl with the lemon slices. Add the lemon rind and juice, olive oil and marjoram, season with salt and pepper and they are then ready to serve. Ideally, they should reach the plate still slightly warm from the cooking.

The dressing in this recipe really pulls the flavours together: sweet artichoke, bitter radicchio and crunchy golden toast. Lovely.

Artichoke salad with lambs' lettuce, croutons & radicchio

– 12 small globe artichokes, stalks attached
– 1 head of radicchio, leaves separated
– 500g (1lb 2oz) lambs' lettuce
– 4 slices of bread
– 50ml (2fl oz) virgin olive oil
– 200ml House dressing (*see* page 297)
– sea salt and pepper

Serves 4–6 | Vegetarian

1 Follow steps 1 and 2 on page 190 to prepare and cook the artichokes. Put the halved artichokes into a large mixing bowl.

2 Preheat the oven to 190°C/fan 170°C/gas mark 5. Prepare a sinkful of cold water and add some ice cubes. Cut the radicchio into bite-sized pieces and drop into the cold water with the lambs' lettuce.

3 Cut the bread slices into rough 2–3cm (3/4–1¼in) cubes, spread out on a baking sheet and drizzle with the olive oil. Bake in the oven for 6–8 minutes, until golden brown, turning once or twice during cooking so that they get an all-over tan. Leave to cool.

4 Drain the lettuce and dry thoroughly, then drop into the artichoke bowl. Add the cooled croutons and gently mix the salad together with the dressing. Adjust the seasoning to taste.

These crispy artichokes, prepared in the Roman way, are a great way to start a meal: fun, inviting and also a good conversation opener.

Artichokes Romani with deep-fried julienne of leeks

- 12 small globe artichokes
- 3 litres (5¼ pints) sunflower oil, for deep-frying
- 3 leeks, white parts only
- 2 lemons, cut into wedges
- sea salt and pepper

Serves 2–4 | Vegetarian

1   Using a small, sharp knife, cut the artichoke stalks to leave about 5cm (2in) of artichoke, then peel the outer leaves away slightly. Gently prise open each artichoke using your fingers, then turn upside down and press to spread the leaves out – the aim is to open them up and slightly flatten them. Season the insides with salt and pepper.

2   Heat the sunflower oil in a deep, heavy-based saucepan to 180°C, or until a cube of bread browns in 30 seconds. Fry the artichokes in batches of 3 for 4 minutes, then remove with a slotted spoon and drain on kitchen paper. Keep the cooked artichokes hot while you fry the remainder.

3   While the artichokes are cooking, cut the leeks in half lengthways. Wash them under cold running water to remove any sand or soil, then drain well and cut into very thin strips (julienne). Use kitchen paper to absorb any excess water. Fry the strips in the hot oil for 1–2 minutes, until golden brown.

4   Serve the artichokes hot with the deep-fried leeks and the lemon wedges. Sprinkle with sea salt before serving.

Avocado
Cucumber
Pepper
Tomato
Sweetcorn
Aubergine
Courgette
Squash
Mushroom

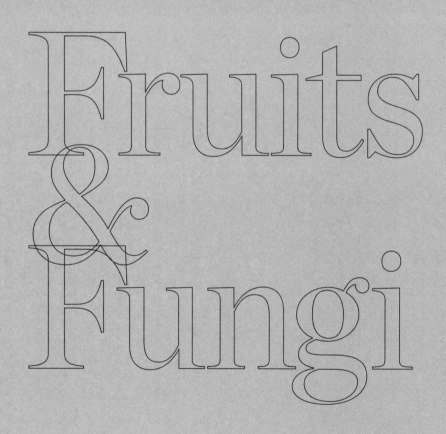

Fruits & Fungi

Super fresh and really creamy, this salad kicks off a meal beautifully. In fact, with a couple of buttered crispbreads, this can be a lovely lunchtime salad.

Avocado salad with wild rocket & pea shoots

- 3 ripe avocados
- 2 bunches of wild rocket
- 150g (5¹/₂oz) pea shoots
- 1 lemon, for squeezing
- 2 tbsp balsamic vinegar
- 75ml (2¹/₂fl oz) olive oil
- salt and pepper

Serves 4–6 | Vegetarian

1   Cut the avocados in half, discard the stones, then cut the halves in half again – it will now be easy to peel off the skin. Cut the flesh into bite-sized chunks.

2   Put a quarter of the avocado pieces in a bowl, then add a handful of rocket and pea shoots, squeeze over a little lemon juice and drizzle over a little of the balsamic vinegar and olive oil. Gently combine with your fingertips and repeat the process with the remaining ingredients in the same order, finishing with the seasoning. Serve immediately.

I like to grill haloumi, but
you can fry it instead if you like.
I love the texture and the squeaky
sound it makes.

Avocado with grilled haloumi & mint

- 200g (7oz) haloumi cheese, drained
- 3 ripe avocados, peeled, stoned and cut into bite-sized chunks
- 1 bunch of mint, chopped
- 2 tbsp balsamic vinegar
- 75ml (2¹/₂fl oz) olive oil
- salt and pepper

Serves 4–6 | Vegetarian

1   Preheat the grill to high. Cut the haloumi into slices 1cm (¹/₂in) thick. Place on a grilling rack and grill for about 5 minutes, until the top becomes deep golden brown – the darker the colour, the more bite the cheese will have when it cools. Turn the haloumi over and grill the other side for 5 minutes, or until the same colour, then remove and leave to cool slightly.

2   Place a few pieces of avocado on a serving plate, then tear the haloumi into bite-sized pieces and add them too. Sprinkle with some of the mint, salt and pepper, vinegar and olive oil. Repeat the layers of avocado, haloumi and flavourings until the ingredients are used up. This is a great way to ensure each mouthful captures the brilliant combination of flavours.

Yes, you can make soup with avocado and it works brilliantly. I serve it hot, but it lends itself very well to being served cold too, as does the cucumber soup. Keep the skin on the cucumbers – they give the second soup its lovely bright green colour.

Avocado soup with crème fraîche

- 50g (1³/₄oz) butter
- 1 large white onion, cut into 3cm (1¹/₄in) cubes
- 1 head of celery, trimmed and cut into 2cm (³/₄in) pieces
- 2 garlic cloves, crushed
- 60g (2¹/₄oz) white long-grain rice
- 1 litre (1³/₄ pints) hot Vegetable stock (*see* page 297)
- 100ml (3¹/₂fl oz) crème fraîche, plus extra to serve
- 3 ripe avocados, peeled, stoned and cut into bite-sized chunks
- 1 lemon, for squeezing
- salt and pepper

Serves 4–6 | Vegetarian

1   Melt the butter in a saucepan, add the onion and cook over a medium heat for 3 minutes without colouring, stirring occasionally. Add the celery and garlic, season with salt and pepper and cook for 15 minutes, stirring occasionally and allowing the vegetables to colour only lightly. Add the rice and cook, stirring, for 5 minutes, then add the hot stock and simmer for 25 minutes. Stir in the crème fraîche and heat through, but don't allow to boil.

2   Transfer the soup in batches to a blender and blend until smooth, adding the avocado as you do so. Pour into a clean saucepan and check the seasoning. Finish the soup with a little lemon juice and reheat gently. Serve hot in bowls with an extra spoonful of crème fraîche added to the centre of each.

Cucumber soup

- 75ml (2¹/₂fl oz) olive oil
- 1 large white onion, cut into 2cm (³/₄in) cubes
- 8 celery sticks, cut into 2cm (³/₄in) pieces
- 2 leeks, trimmed, washed and cut into 2cm (³/₄in) pieces
- 2 garlic cloves, crushed
- 1 large potato, peeled and cut into 4cm (1¹/₂in) cubes
- 1 litre (1³/₄ pints) hot Vegetable stock (*see* page 297)
- 2 cucumbers
- 150ml (¹/₄ pint) double cream
- 1 lemon, for squeezing
- salt and pepper

Serves 4–6 | Vegetarian

1   Heat the olive oil in a saucepan, add the onion and cook over a medium heat for 3 minutes without colouring, stirring occasionally. Add the celery, leeks and garlic, season with salt and pepper and cook for 15 minutes, stirring occasionally, allowing the vegetables to colour only lightly. Add the potato and cook for 5 minutes, stirring frequently, then add the hot stock and simmer for 20 minutes. Meanwhile, cut 6 thin discs from the centre of one of the cucumbers and reserve for garnishing, then top and tail the cucumbers and cut the remainder into 3–4cm (1¹/₄–1¹/₂in) pieces.

2   Add the cucumber to the vegetable pan, return the soup to the boil and simmer for another 5 minutes, by which time the potato should be cooked. Turn off the heat and stir in the cream. Transfer the soup in batches to a blender and blend until smooth. Check the seasoning and add a touch of lemon juice to lift the cucumber flavour even further. Serve either hot or cold, garnished with the reserved cucumber slices.

Fish sauce may seem an unlikely ingredient but this recipe sings from the heavens because of the addition of it. The mint freshens up the whole salad and the chilli gives it fire. The combination of ingredients is one you may never have tried, but I reckon this salad will become a regular in your culinary repertoire.

Cucumber, watermelon & mango salad

- **400g (14oz) cucumber**
- **400g (14oz) watermelon**
- **400g (14oz) mango**
- **3 tbsp roughly chopped mint, plus extra mint leaves to serve**
- **1 fresh red chilli, thinly sliced into rings**
- **1 fresh green chilli, thinly sliced into rings**
- **3 tsp Thai fish sauce**
- **3 tsp mirin (rice wine)**
- **75ml (2½fl oz) olive oil**
- **salt and pepper**

Serves 4–6

1   Peel the cucumber, then cut in half lengthways and scoop out the seeds. Chop the flesh into bite-sized chunks and put them into a large mixing bowl.

2   Peel the watermelon then cut the flesh into bite-sized chunks. Add to the bowl. Peel the mango, then cut the flesh away from the thin central stone. Chop into bite-sized pieces and add to the bowl.

3   Add the chopped mint and chillies to the bowl, then the fish sauce and mirin. Drizzle in the olive oil and season lightly with salt and pepper. Mix the salad well, then arrange it in bowls or on plates and serve with a few more delicate mint leaves on top.

This is slightly in homage to the 1980s, when cucumber fans were the garnish for almost everything, but I like the colour contrast, and once you start making the fans, hey, you might never stop.

Chilled red pepper soup with cucumber fans

- 30g (1oz) butter
- 75ml (2½fl oz) olive oil
- 1 large white onion, cut into 2cm (¾in) cubes
- 2kg (4lb 8oz) red peppers, deseeded and cut into 2cm (¾in) pieces
- 8 celery sticks, cut into 2cm (¾in) pieces
- 1 fresh red chilli, deseeded and finely chopped
- 2 garlic cloves, crushed
- 60g (2¼oz) white long-grain rice
- 1 litre (1¾oz) hot Vegetable stock (*see* page 297)
- 200ml (7fl oz) milk
- 1 lemon, for squeezing
- 1 cucumber
- sea salt and pepper

Serves 4–6 | Vegetarian

1   Melt the butter with the olive oil in a saucepan, add the onion and cook over a medium heat for 3 minutes without colouring, stirring occasionally. Add the red peppers, celery, chilli and garlic, season with salt and pepper and cook for 15 minutes, stirring occasionally. Add the rice and cook, stirring, for 5 minutes, then add the hot stock and simmer for 20 minutes. Turn off the heat, stir in the milk and add a squeeze of lemon juice to taste.

2   Transfer the soup in batches to a blender and blend until smooth, or keep it chunky if you like. Pour it into a bowl and leave to cool, then cover with clingfilm and chill in the refrigerator for at least 2 hours.

3   For the cucumber fans, top and tail the cucumber, then cut into blocks 6cm (2½in) long. Cut each block lengthways into 6 pieces, making sure that each piece has an equal amount of green skin showing on the outside. Cut out the seeds and round off the green corners. Lay each piece, skin-side up, on a chopping board. Make a series of very close cuts through the skin, leaving one end uncut to hold the slices together. Fan out the slices with your thumb. Serve the chilled soup in bowls with the cucumber fans arranged on top.

Believe me, the flavours of this dish are as dazzling as the colours. You can eat it hot, at room temperature or chilled – all three ways are equally delicious. You can reverse the idea with the oxheart tomatoes version.

Stuffed red peppers with thyme, garlic & anchovies

- **6 red peppers**
- **600g (1lb 5oz) tomatoes in a mixture of colours**
- **leaves from 1 bunch of thyme**
- **3 garlic cloves, chopped**
- **24 anchovy fillets**
- **100ml (3½fl oz) olive oil**
- **½ handful of baby basil leaves**
- **salt and pepper**

Serves 4–6

1   Preheat the oven to 180°C/fan 160°C/gas mark 4. Cut each red pepper in half lengthways through the stalk. Pick out the seeds and white cores and lay the pepper halves on a roasting tray, open-side up.

2   Cut the tomatoes into bite-sized pieces and put them into a mixing bowl. Add most of the thyme leaves, and all the garlic to the bowl, season with salt and pepper and mix well. Spoon the tomato mixture into the pepper cavities and top each stuffed pepper with an anchovy fillet. Drizzle the stuffed peppers evenly with the olive oil and roast for 25–30 minutes. Sprinkle the reserved thyme and basil leaves over the top and serve.

Stuffed oxheart tomatoes

Cut 6 big oxheart tomatoes (or any other large tomato) and 6 red peppers in half horizontally and discard all the seeds. Chop the peppers into small chunks and combine with the herbs, anchovies and garlic as above. Stuff 6 tomato halves with the pepper mixture, top with the remaining halves and drizzle over the olive oil. Roast in the oven as above and sprinkle the remaining thyme and basil leaves over the top before serving.

This is a lovely way to preserve peppers if you have a few too many, but they end up so delicious that they'll be eaten before you can even think about sitting them on a shelf.

Marinated baby peppers with mustard seed & bay

- 24 baby red, orange and yellow peppers
- 12 bay leaves
- 3 tbsp yellow mustard seeds
- 750ml (1¼ pints) olive oil

Makes 1 small (500 ml) jar | Vegetarian

1   Sterilize a large Kilner-type jar (follow step 3 of the method on page 180).

2   Bring another large saucepan of water to the boil, drop in the peppers and blanch for 3 minutes. Drain, dry quickly with kitchen paper and place in the sterilized jar, intermittently adding the bay leaves and mustard seeds as you fill the jar. Pour the olive oil over the peppers, making sure they are fully covered by the oil, then seal. Store in a cool, dark place for 2 weeks – but not in the refrigerator, as the olive oil will go cloudy – and they are ready to go. They will keep, unopened, for up to 2 months in cool, dark conditions. Once opened, refrigerate and use within 2 weeks.

This is such a creative way to put a salad together. Passing an egg through a sieve might not seem normal, but it makes the finished dish so pretty and delicious. Don't tell your guests how you made this salad – see if they can guess.

Blackened red pepper salad with grated egg & anchovy

- 6 large red peppers
- 6 tbsp olive oil
- 3 free-range eggs, hard-boiled
- 12 anchovy fillets
- 3 tbsp finely chopped flat leaf parsley
- salt and pepper

Serves 4–6

1   Preheat the oven to 220°C/fan 200°C/gas mark 7. Rub the red peppers with 2 tablespoons of the olive oil, then arrange them on a roasting tray and roast for 20–25 minutes, turning once or twice during cooking so that the skins are evenly scorched.

2   Transfer the roasted peppers to a large bowl. Cover with clingfilm to seal in the heat and steam, and then leave to cool. Meanwhile, shell the eggs and reserve.

3   Peel the peppers – the skin should come away easily. Discard the stalks, all the seeds and membrane. Flatten the pepper flesh on a serving platter and arrange the anchovy fillets all over them.

4   Separate the egg yolks from the whites. Hold a sieve over the serving platter and press the whites through the sieve so that they fall on the red pepper and look almost like snow, lightly covering the whole plate. Then press the egg yolks through the sieve over the salad. Sprinkle lightly with parsley, drizzle over the remaining olive oil and serve.

Skill: Tomato sauce

Tomato sauce is so versatile – and so easy to make – that you'll use this method again and again. Remember, the longer the cooking the sweeter the sauce, so I cook it for as long as possible without it drying out in the pan. For a slightly smoother texture, blanch the tomatoes first and then peel off the skins.

Penne arrabiata with pecorino

- **650g (1lb 7oz) dried penne**
- **salt and pepper**
- **freshly grated pecorino cheese, to serve**

Arrabiata sauce
- **100ml (3¹/₂fl oz) olive oil**
- **4 garlic cloves**
- **1kg (2lb 4oz) soft ripe tomatoes**
- **1kg (2lb 4oz) cherry tomatoes**
- **1–2 fresh red chillies**
- **1 large bunch of basil**
- **2 tsp dried red chilli flakes**

Serves 6 | Vegetarian

1   For the sauce, pour 50ml (2fl oz) of the olive oil into a high-sided frying pan to cover the base and heat through over a medium heat. Peel the garlic, then slice very thinly, add to the pan and cook for 1–2 minutes, stirring gently, until it is a light golden colour, being careful not to let it burn.

2   Chop the regular tomatoes into 4cm (1¹/₂in) chunks, add them to the pan and cook for 10 minutes, stirring frequently. While the tomatoes are cooking, chop the cherry tomatoes, and deseed and very finely chop the fresh chillies. Add the cherry tomatoes to the pan and cook for a further 10 minutes, stirring frequently. Meanwhile, pick the leaves from half the bunch of basil and finely chop. Add the basil to the pan with the fresh chillies and chilli flakes, increase the heat to high and crush the tomatoes into a sauce. When the sauce is bubbling nicely, reduce the heat to a very low simmer, season with 2 teaspoons salt and pepper to taste and cook for 30 minutes, or 40 minutes for an even sweeter, deep flavour, stirring occasionally.

3   Drizzle in the remaining olive oil and add the rest of the basil, finely chopped, reserving 6 whole leaves for garnish. Cook for 5 minutes more, check the seasoning and the sauce is ready to use.

4   While the sauce finishes cooking, cook the penne in a large saucepan of salted boiling water for 10–12 minutes, or according to the packet instructions, until al dente. Drain the cooked penne, reserving 2–3 tablespoons of the pasta cooking water. Mix the pasta into half the sauce with the cooking water, reserving the remaining sauce to top the dish. Serve sprinkled with grated pecorino and garnished with the reserved basil leaves.

Classic tomato sauce

- 2kg (4lb 8oz) soft ripe tomatoes
- 100ml (3½fl oz) olive oil
- 1 tsp dried red chilli flakes
- 4 garlic cloves, very thinly sliced
- salt and pepper

Serves 6 | Vegetarian

1   Plunge the tomatoes into boiling water and leave for 15 seconds, then lift out with a slotted spoon into cold water – the skins will then peel off easily. Chop the tomatoes.

2   Pour the olive oil into a high-sided frying pan to cover the base and heat through over a medium heat. Add the chilli flakes and garlic and cook for 3–4 minutes until the garlic is pale golden brown, stirring occasionally. Add the tomatoes, increase the heat to high and crush the tomatoes into a sauce. When the sauce is bubbling nicely, reduce the heat to a very low simmer, season with salt and pepper and cook for 30 minutes, stirring occasionally.

Celeriac lasagne with broccoli & Parmesan

- 100ml (3½fl oz) olive oil
- 2kg (4lb 8oz) celeriac, peeled and thinly sliced
- 600g (1lb 5oz) dried lasagne sheets
- 600g (1lb 5oz) broccoli, cut into florets
- 1 quantity Arrabiata sauce (see page 208)
- 1 quantity Béchamel sauce (see page 297)
- 150g (5½oz) Parmesan, freshly grated
- salt and pepper

Serves 6 | Vegetarian

1   Preheat the oven to 160°C/fan 140°C/gas mark 3. Drizzle some of the olive oil into the base of a high-sided roasting tray. First add a layer of celeriac, then a layer each of lasagne sheets, broccoli, the tomato sauce, béchamel sauce and Parmesan, seasoning the layers with salt and pepper as you go. Repeat the same layering of ingredients until they are used up but making sure you finish with a final layering of celeriac, then béchamel sauce and finally Parmesan.

2   Drizzle with the remaining olive oil and bake for 2 hours. Remove from the oven and serve straight away with a lovely dressed side salad.

Pumpkin farfalle with paprika & tomatoes

- 100ml (3½ml) olive oil
- 1.25kg (2lb 12oz) pumpkin, peeled, deseeded and thinly sliced
- 1 quantity Classic tomato sauce (see left)
- 4 tbsp chopped basil
- 1 quantity Béchamel sauce (see page 297)
- 600g (1lb 5oz) dried farfalle
- 150g (5½oz) Parmesan cheese, freshly grated
- 2 tsp paprika
- salt and pepper

Serves 6 | Vegetarian

1   Preheat the oven to 160°C/fan 140°C/gas mark 3. Drizzle some of the olive oil into the base of a high-sided roasting tray. First add a layer of pumpkin, then a layer each of the tomato sauce topped with a sprinkling of the basil, the béchamel sauce, farfalle and Parmesan, seasoning the layers with the paprika and salt and pepper as you go. Repeat the same layering of ingredients until they are used up but making sure you finish with a final layering of pumpkin, then béchamel sauce and finally Parmesan.

2   Drizzle with the remaining olive oil and bake for 2 hours. Remove from the oven and serve straight away.

Cauliflower bake with aubergine & peppers

- 2 pale aubergines
- 150ml (¼ pint) olive oil
- 3 red peppers
- 600g (1lb 5oz) cauliflower, cut into florets
- 1 quantity Arrabiata sauce (see page 208)
- 1 quantity Béchamel sauce (see page 297)
- 200g (7oz) Parmesan cheese, freshly grated
- salt and pepper

Serves 6 | Vegetarian

1   Preheat the oven to 180°C/fan 160°C/gas mark 4. Top and tail the aubergines, then cut them into 3cm (1¼in) thick discs. Heat 75ml (2½fl oz) of the olive oil in a large frying pan over a medium-high heat. Fry the aubergine discs, in batches, for about 5 minutes on each side until golden. Remove from the pan, drain on kitchen paper and reserve. While the aubergine is cooking, cut the peppers into quarters, and remove the stalks, seeds and cores.

2   Add a little more of the olive oil to the frying pan, add the peppers and cook over a medium heat for 6 minutes, turning occasionally, until tender. Remove from the pan and keep warm.

3   Drizzle some of the remaining olive oil into the base of a high-sided roasting tray. First add a layer of cauliflower, then a layer each of aubergine, the tomato sauce, béchamel sauce, red pepper and Parmesan, seasoning the layers lightly with salt and pepper as you go. Repeat the same layering of ingredients until they are used up but making sure you finish with a final layering of cauliflower, then béchamel sauce and finally Parmesan.

4   Drizzle with the remaining olive oil and bake for 1 hour. Remove from the oven and serve straight away.

Roasted aubergine tower with spinach & tomato

- 3 pale aubergines
- 600g (1lb 5oz) spinach, washed and drained
- 150ml (¼ pint) olive oil
- 1 quantity Classic tomato sauce (see left)
- 200g (7oz) goats' cheese
- 150g (5½oz) wild rocket
- juice of 1 lemon
- salt and pepper

Serves 6 | Vegetarian

1   Top and tail the aubergines, then cut them into 2cm (¾in) thick discs. Place in a sieve and very lightly sprinkle with salt.

2   Cook the spinach in a saucepan of salted boiling water for 3–4 minutes, then drain well and leave to cool to room temperature, drizzling over a little of the olive oil while it is cooling.

3   Preheat the oven to 180°C/fan 160°C/gas mark 4. Heat a little of the olive oil in a large frying pan over a medium-high heat. Fry the aubergine discs, in batches, for about 5 minutes on each side. Remove from the pan and drain on kitchen paper.

4   Place an aubergine disc on a roasting tray and add some of the spinach so that it entirely covers the top of the aubergine. Spoon some of the tomato sauce on to the spinach, covering it completely. Top with another aubergine disc and repeat the same layering of ingredients, finishing with an aubergine disc. Spoon over a little more tomato sauce and cut a disc of goats' cheese to go on top of the tower. Repeat with the remaining ingredients, reserving a little of the tomato sauce for serving. Bake the towers for 15 minutes, or until the top of the goats' cheese is golden and crisp.

5   To serve, dress the rocket with the remaining olive oil and lemon juice, then gently arrange a handful on top of each tower for a striking presentation, spooning a little of the tomato sauce around the outside edge of each tower.

Marjoram and tomatoes are such an amazing combination, you could almost be convinced that it works better than basil and tomatoes. Try it – you might never look back.

Heritage tomato salad with marjoram

- 1kg (2lb 4oz) tomatoes in a mixture of colours
- 2 garlic cloves, very finely chopped
- 3 tbsp marjoram leaves
- 3 tbsp herb vinegar
- 4 tbsp olive oil, plus extra for drizzling
- 12 slices of French bread stick, cut into croutons and toasted
- 100g (3½oz) Parmesan cheese
- salt and pepper
- golden marjoram sprigs, to garnish

Serves 4–6 | Vegetarian

1   Cut the tomatoes into bite-sized pieces of different shapes and put them into a mixing bowl. Add the garlic and marjoram leaves and season with salt and pepper, then add the vinegar and olive oil and mix well. Leave the salad to sit at room temperature for at least 30 minutes before serving. This really helps the flavours to develop.

2   When ready to serve, mix the croutons through the salad and arrange on serving plates. Using a knife or a peeler, shave delicate strips of the Parmesan on top of each salad, then drizzle over a tiny bit more olive oil and garnish with golden marjoram. Serve straight away.

Golden, crisp, warm and delicious – what more could you want than toasted ciabbata drizzled with extra virgin olive oil and topped with sea salt? Well, roasted tomatoes, red peppers and garlic, all sweet from a slow spell in the oven and made wonderfully summery by basil and marjoram, that's what!

Baked tomato, garlic & red pepper crostini

- **400g (14oz) tomatoes, chopped**
- **1 red pepper, halved**
- **2 garlic bulbs**
- **1 banana shallot, finely diced**
- **75ml (2¹/₂fl oz) virgin olive oil**
- **2 tbsp chopped basil**
- **1 tbsp chopped marjoram**
- **1 ciabatta loaf**
- **sea salt, for sprinkling**
- **wild rocket, to garnish**
- **salt and pepper**

Makes 6 | Vegetarian

1   Preheat the oven to 160°C/fan 140°C/gas mark 2. Arrange the tomato and red pepper on a roasting tray. Cut 1 garlic bulb horizontally in half and place the 2 halves, cut-side up, on the tray. Separate the cloves from the other bulb and scatter on the tray. Sprinkle the shallot over the vegetables, drizzle in half the olive oil, add the chopped herbs and season with salt and pepper. Roast for about 1 hour, until soft and browned.

2   Near the end of the roasting time, cut the ciabatta into 6 slices and place them on a baking sheet. Drizzle with the remaining olive oil and sprinkle lightly with sea salt.

3   Remove the roasting tray from the oven and leave to cool. Increase the temperature to 180°C/fan 160°C/gas mark 4, place the ciabatta in the oven and watch them turn golden – and I do mean watch them, as turning your back on the crostini invariably results in them toasting too much. I like my crostini golden on the top but slightly soft in the middle, creating a lovely chewy centre when the moist toppings go on.

4   Working quickly, pick up the garlic cloves and squeeze the roasted flesh on to 2 of the crostini – have no fear, as the garlic is now mellow and delicious. Spoon the tomatoes on to 2 more of the crostini. Peel the red pepper, discarding the stalk, seeds and membrane and pulling the flesh into strips as you go. Arrange the strips of pepper on the remaining 2 crostini. Spoon over the herby, shalloty juices from the roasting tray and decorate with the rocket. Serve slightly warm.

Here is a really creative way of combining tomatoes with beef, or even with meaty fish such as tuna. The meat is encased in chopped tomatoes and slow-cooks – almost steaming inside the pile – ending up being really moist. It's great the next day too.

Tomato confit with beef

- 750g (1lb 10oz) piece of fillet of beef, trimmed of any fat or sinew
- 2kg (4lb 8oz) tomatoes in a mixture of colours
- 3 garlic cloves, chopped
- 3 tbsp marjoram leaves
- 100ml (3^1/2fl oz) olive oil, plus 2 tbsp for drizzling
- salt and pepper

Serves 4–6

1   Season the beef well with salt and pepper and let it come to room temperature. Cut the tomatoes into bite-sized pieces and put them into a mixing bowl. Add the garlic, marjoram and the 100ml (3^1/2fl oz) olive oil to the bowl and season well. Mix well and reserve.

2   Preheat the oven to 180°C/fan 160°C/gas mark 4. Take a large handful of the tomato mixture and place in a mound in the centre of a large, deep roasting tray. Place the beef on top of the mound, making sure there is at least 4cm (1^1/2in) of tomato between the tray and the meat. Now cover the beef with the rest of the tomatoes, creating a large pile.

3   Roast for 15 minutes, then open the oven and spoon the cooking liquid over the tomatoes, then remove and discard some of the liquid to prevent the meat stewing. Return the pan to the oven to roast for 15 minutes. Repeat this process then continue to roast for another 15 minutes. Cook for at least 45 minutes in total for a lovely rosy pink centre to the beef, or longer if preferred. To check the degree of doneness, move any tomatoes to one side and push a skewer into the centre of the beef. Count to 10 and remove the skewer. Check the temperature of the skewer with your fingertip, and if not too hot, place the skewer on your palm. If the skewer is the temperature of your palm, the beef is still very pink; if the skewer feels fairly hot, the beef will be lightly pink. If the skewer is very hot, the beef will be well done.

4   When the beef is cooked to your liking, leave the tray to rest for 10 minutes. Spoon away the tomatoes, cut the beef into generous slices and arrange on serving plates. Drizzle the 2 tablespoons of olive oil over the tomatoes and serve with the beef.

Everywhere I go people ask me to cook these delicate little pancakes, so I thought I would give everyone the recipe so they can make them themselves. The reason they work so well is down to the sweetness of the raw sweetcorn. Serve them with a dressed salad.

Sweetcorn & coriander pikelets

- 4 free-range eggs, separated
- 900g (2lb) sweetcorn kernels, cut from the cob
- 280ml (9¹/₂fl oz) milk
- 1 tbsp melted butter, plus extra butter to serve
- 115g (4oz) plain flour
- ¹/₂ tsp salt
- 1 fresh red chilli, deseeded and finely chopped
- 3 tbsp chopped coriander
- light olive oil, for cooking

Serves 4–6 | Vegetarian

1   Break the eggs into a bowl and lift out the yolks to separate them from the egg whites. Beat the egg yolks in a small mixing bowl, then add to the sweetcorn kernels in a large mixing bowl. Stir in the milk and melted butter, then add the flour, salt, chilli and coriander and beat well.

2   Whisk the egg whites in a large, grease-free mixing bowl until they hold firm peaks, then fold into the sweetcorn mixture.

3   Heat a little light olive oil in a frying pan over a medium-high heat. Dollop in separate tablespoonfuls of the sweetcorn mixture and cook for about 3 minutes on each side until well browned. Serve hot with a knob of butter for your guests to melt over each of the pikelets themselves.

Pea & mint pikelets

Prepare the batter as above, substituting the sweetcorn with the same amount of fresh peas, and replacing the coriander with the same amount of mint.

I tried this dish in America and promised myself that I'd put the recipe in this book. So here it is in all its glorious simplicity. For an added kick, mix in a teaspoonful of chopped fresh chilli.

Creamed sweetcorn

- **6 corn cobs**
- **100g (3 1/2oz) butter**
- **1 large white onion, finely chopped**
- **300ml (1/2 pint) double cream**
- **salt and pepper**

Serves 4–6 | Vegetarian

1   Peel the green husks from the corn cobs and remove the silky threads. Take a cob and hold it by the stalk end, angled slightly away from you, and slice downwards and away from you, in a large, deep bowl, to cut away the kernels. Do this with each cob.

2   Melt the butter in a saucepan, add the onion and cook over a medium heat for about 6 minutes, until translucent, stirring frequently.

3   Add the sweetcorn kernels to the pan and cook the mixture for 12 minutes, stirring occasionally. Add the cream and bring to the boil, then turn off the heat, check the seasoning and serve hot.

Creamed sweetcorn with lardons

For another dimension, put 200g (7oz) pancetta lardons in a hot frying pan and cook for 3 minutes over a medium heat. Leave to cool. Make the creamed corn as above, then drain the oil from the lardons and add them to the sweetcorn mixture. Check the seasoning and serve hot. For even more depth of flavour, finely chop 1 clove of smoked garlic, and add it to the dish before serving.

I try not to use the mass-produced dark purple variety for my aubergine dishes. I feel they have lost some of their character. Instead, I opt for the larger pale aubergines that you can find in so many food markets nowadays. If you don't use up all the ratatouille, refrigerate it and it will taste even better the next day, as the flavours will have had more time to combine.

Ratatouille with basil & extra virgin olive oil

- **500g (1lb 2oz) pale aubergines, cut into 1cm (1/2in) cubes**
- **500g (1lb 2oz) yellow courgettes**
- **500g (1lb 2oz) red peppers, deseeded and cut into 1cm (1/2in) pieces**
- **500g (1lb 2oz) tomatoes, quartered**
- **150ml (1/4 pint) extra virgin olive oil**
- **2 garlic cloves, finely chopped**
- **2 tbsp finely chopped basil**
- **salt and pepper**

Serves 4–6 | Vegetarian

1   Put the aubergines, courgettes and peppers into separate containers. Remove the seeds and pulp from half of the tomatoes and put into a blender. Blend the seeds and pulp to a purée. Pass it through a sieve and set aside. Cut the flesh that remains and all the remaining tomatoes into 1cm (1/2in) dice.

2   Heat a large frying pan over a medium-high heat and, when hot, add some of the aubergine, making sure you don't add too much at one time, as the aim is to fry each piece rather than boiling them in their own juices. Once the aubergine is in the pan, add just enough of the olive oil to fry it. Fry for 3–4 minutes, until golden brown, stirring occasionally. Lightly season with salt and pepper, then tip into a large sieve to allow the excess oil to drip away. Continue frying the remaining vegetables in batches, adding each fried batch to the sieve. When all done, discard the oil and juices, as these will be bitter.

3   Once all the vegetables are fried, wipe the pan clean, add 2 tablespoons of the olive oil and fry the garlic over a medium heat for about 2 minutes, stirring frequently, until lightly golden. Add the basil and cook, stirring, for 2 minutes before adding the tomato purée. Bring to the boil then add all the fried vegetables. Reduce the heat and gently cook the ratatouille for 15 minutes, stirring it lightly but often to really mix the flavours together. Check the seasoning and serve. Alternatively, sterilize a Kilner-type jar (*see* step 3, page 180), fill with the ratatouille, then seal and store for up to 2 months in a cool, dark place.

If you can't find wasabi (Japanese horseradish) for the mayonnaise, you could substitute English mustard, and if the tempura is for the kids, just cut out the wasabi altogether.

Aubergine tempura with wasabi mayonnaise

– 1kg (2lb 4oz) aubergines, sliced into discs 1cm (1/2in) thick
– 3 litres (5¼ pints) sunflower oil, for deep-frying
– plain flour, for dusting
– 500ml (18fl oz) Tempura batter (*see* page 297)
– 50g (1³/4oz) wasabi paste, or to taste
– 150g (5¹/2oz) Homemade mayonnaise (*see* page 297)
– sea salt

Serves 4–6 | Vegetarian

1   Heat the sunflower oil in a deep, heavy-based saucepan to 180°C, or until a cube of bread browns in 30 seconds. Dust the aubergine discs in flour – this helps the batter stick to them – and pat off any excess. Dip them into the batter and allow any excess to drip off. Carefully lower a battered disc in the hot oil, making sure that you don't drop it in, then add 2 more discs, which will probably fill the pan. Fry for 2 minutes, then turn the discs over and fry for a further 2 minutes. You are aiming for a very light, golden crisp covering to your aubergine, so if they have not coloured or crisped up, fry for a little while longer. Remove with a slotted spoon and drain on kitchen paper. Keep hot while you fry the remaining aubergine discs.

2   While the aubergines are frying, mix the wasabi paste with the Homemade mayonnaise – you can add as much or as little wasabi as you like. Serve the aubergine tempura hot, sprinkled with sea salt and each serving topped with a spoonful of the wasabi mayonnaise.

Cooking aubergine slowly makes them so creamy, and with slow-cooked tomatoes on top, this dish hits new heights. The salsa gets hotter the longer you store it – leave for 48 hours and you will have the most delicious, kick-ass sauce ever. You absolutely must try this recipe.

Shallow-fried aubergine with salsa rossa

- 1kg (2lb 4oz) pale aubergines, sliced into discs 2cm (³/₄in) thick

Salsa rossa
- 600g (1lb 5oz) red peppers
- 3 fresh red chillies
- 100ml (3¹/₂fl oz) light olive oil
- 2 garlic cloves, very thinly sliced
- 600g (1lb 5oz) tomatoes, peeled, deseeded and chopped
- salt and pepper

Serves 4–6 | Vegetarian

1   Preheat the oven to 200°C/fan 180°C/gas mark 6. Place the aubergines in a sieve and sprinkle very lightly with salt.

2   Arrange the red peppers and chillies on a roasting tray and roast for 25 minutes. Remove from the oven, place in a large bowl and cover immediately with clingfilm to seal in the heat and steam. Leave until the vegetables and pan are cool, about 20 minutes.

3   Meanwhile, heat 2 tablespoons of the olive oil in a saucepan, add the garlic and fry gently for 3–4 minutes, stirring frequently, until lightly golden. Add the tomatoes, press down on them and mix well with the oil and garlic. Season lightly with salt and pepper and leave to cook over a medium heat for 25 minutes, stirring occasionally.

4   Peel the peppers and chillies – the skin should come away easily, then discard the stalks, seeds and membrane as best you can – the heat of a chilli is concentrated in the seeds and membrane, so if you leave them in, you will have an even hotter salsa. Strain any liquid left in the bowl to remove any burnt or seedy bits and reserve. Chop the pepper flesh into 1cm (¹/₂in) pieces and put them into a large bowl. Cut the chillies into long, fine strips and add them to the peppers. Check the seasoning of the tomatoes, then add into the pepper and chilli mixture. Add the reserved liquid and check the seasoning one last time. Mix well, cover the bowl with clingfilm and place in the refrigerator until ready to serve.

5   Heat the remaining olive oil in a large frying pan over a medium-high heat. Fry the aubergine discs in batches, for 6–8 minutes on each side, until well browned. Serve warm, topped with spoonfuls of salsa rossa.

Here the aubergine is roasted with all of the ingredients mixed through. Some pieces will turn darker than others, but the combined flavours of the dark and light aubergine work brilliantly.

Aubergine, parsley & lemon crostini

- 1kg (2lb 4oz) aubergines, a mixture of dark and pale
- 150ml (¼ pint) olive oil, plus extra for drizzling
- 1 unwaxed lemon
- 6 slices of sourdough bread
- 3 tbsp finely chopped flat-leaf parsley
- salt and pepper

Serves 4–6 | Vegetarian

1   Preheat the oven to 180°C/fan 160°C/gas mark 4. Cut the aubergines into 2cm (¾in) cubes. Place in a sieve and very lightly sprinkle with salt. Set aside for 5 minutes.

2   Lightly rinse the salt from the aubergine cubes and pat dry with kitchen paper. Put them into a large mixing bowl. Add in 100ml (3½fl oz) of the olive oil and the finely grated rind of the lemon, and season lightly with salt and pepper. Mix well. Spread the aubergine cubes out on a roasting tray and roast for 15–20 minutes. Meanwhile, slice the bread into large, thin pieces. Arrange them on a baking sheet and put them into the oven for the last few minutes of the aubergine roasting time to crisp them up.

3   Remove from the crostini from the oven and drizzle over the remaining olive oil. Remove the aubergine from the oven, squeeze the lemon over it and mix lightly with a spoon. Arrange the crostini on serving plates, spoon over the roasted aubergine and sprinkle with the chopped parsley. Serve warm with a drizzle of olive oil.

Salmoriglio is a rich, deeply herby sauce that goes well with grilled vegetables and meat. Essentially, it's a very basic pesto, and carries the punchy flavour of oregano really well. You can make it from almost any herb, but I think oregano is the best.

Chargrilled aubergine with oregano salmoriglio

- 1kg (2lb 4oz) pale aubergines, cut into discs 2cm (3/4in) thick
- 1 bunch of oregano, leaves picked
- juice of 1 lemon
- 150ml (1/4 pint) olive oil
- salt and pepper

Serves 4–6 | Vegetarian

1   Place the aubergines in a sieve and sprinkle very lightly with salt. Set aside.

2   Prepare a charcoal barbecue and make sure that it is fairly hot (the charcoals should have a covering of white ash). Alternatively heat a griddle pan until very hot. Put the oregano leaves into a mortar, sprinkle in a little salt, the pound with a pestle. Once you have a dark green paste, add the lemon juice and mix well, then add the olive oil and mix again.

3   Lightly rinse the salt from the aubergine discs, pat dry on kitchen paper, then place on the barbecue rack. Cook for 10 minutes, moving them once to ensure even cooking. Turn the discs over and cook for another 10 minutes. Alternatively, place the discs on the griddle pan and brown on both sides. Spoon over the salmoriglio while the aubergine is still cooking, and after another 5 minutes, transfer the aubergine on to a serving plate. Serve warm.

Feast: Tex-Mex Grill

This feast is perfect for any grilling-outside-on-a-summer-evening occasion. Not only do the veg take incredibly well to the smoke and heat of grilling, but they work brilliantly with spices, and these dishes really show what you can do with the Texan-Mexican flavours and aromas. The Bean chilli tacos are super fresh: each layer of ingredients adds to the next. Lime & chilli guacamole is one of the easiest dishes in the world. Chargrilled corn has such an amazing smoky flavour, and yellow courgettes and asparagus both chargrill brilliantly. The quesadillas are great fun – drop in a few extra jalapeño peppers if you like. The Sweet potato chips are perfect for sharing. Serve with salsa rossa, lime wedges and pickles.

Tex-Mex Grill

1 Bean chilli tacos

- 600g (1lb 5oz) fresh borlotti beans, podded weight
- 2 garlic cloves
- 1 red onion, finely diced
- 1 tsp dried red chilli flakes
- 1 tbsp red wine vinegar
- 6 taco shells
- 2 tbsp olive oil
- 1 quantity Salsa rossa (see page 226)
- 150g (5½oz) soured cream
- salt and pepper
- guacamole, to serve (see below)

Serves 4–6 | Vegetarian

1 Put the borlotti beans, garlic cloves, onion, chilli flakes and vinegar into a saucepan and cover with fresh cold water to a depth of about 7cm (2¾in). Bring to the boil, then reduce the heat and simmer for 1 hour 20 minutes, or until the beans are completely soft to the bite.

2 When the beans are ready, heat the taco shells according to the packet instructions. Season the beans with salt and pepper, then drain, reserving a quarter of the cooking water. Mash them very roughly with a fork, adding some of the cooking water and the olive oil. Spoon the bean mixture into the warm taco shells, add some guacamole, drizzle over some of the salsa and top each with a spoonful of soured cream.

2 Lime & chilli guacamole

- 1 garlic clove, cut in half
- 2 ripe avocados, cut into chunks
- 1 small red onion, finely chopped
- 1 red tomato, finely diced
- 2 tsp chopped fresh red chilli
- juice of 2 limes
- 2 tbsp finely chopped coriander
- 3 tbsp olive oil
- salt and pepper
- lime wedges, to serve

Serves 4–6 | Vegetarian

1 Use a large pestle and mortar to make the guacamole, but if you don't have one, a large bowl and a rolling pin will do. Rub the inside of the mortar or bowl with the garlic halves.

2 Add the avocado and pound with the pestle or the end of the rolling pin. Add the onion, tomato, chilli, lime juice and half the coriander, season well with salt and pepper and drizzle in the olive oil. Mix the guacamole now rather than pounding it further and add the remaining coriander before serving.

3 Chargrilled corn cobs in their jackets

- 6 corn cobs
- 200g (7oz) butter, plus extra to serve
- salt and pepper

Serves 4–6 | Vegetarian

1 Prepare a charcoal barbecue (see step 2, page 228). Meanwhile, immerse the corn cobs in a large saucepan of boiling water and cook for 5 minutes.

2 When the barbecue is nice and hot, arrange the corn cobs on the rack and cook for 6–8 minutes, turning every couple of minutes, until the husks are well blackened – the smoke from the outer leaves permeates the cobs and the steam cooks them to perfection.

3 Remove a cob from the barbecue, open up the leaves and drop a good piece of butter into it. Season with salt and pepper. Repeat with the remaining cobs. Serve hot with extra butter.

4 Yellow courgettes with herb vinegar & chilli

- 3 large yellow courgettes, sliced lengthways
- 3 tbsp finely chopped mint
- 1 fresh red chilli, finely chopped
- 2 tbsp herb vinegar
- 3 tbsp olive oil
- sea salt and pepper

Serves 4–6 | Vegetarian

1 Lightly sprinkle the courgette slices evenly with sea salt, season with pepper and leave to sit for 20 minutes at room temperature. Meanwhile prepare a charcoal barbecue (see step 2, page 228).

2 Pat the courgette slices dry, then sprinkle over the mint followed by the chilli. Drizzle over the herb vinegar and olive oil, mix together and cook on the preheated barbecue for 10 minutes, turning once. Serve warm.

5 Spicy quesadillas with green jalapeño chillies

- 12 soft flour tortillas
- 300g (10½oz) cream cheese
- 500g (1lb 2oz) Cheddar cheese, grated
- 6 pickled green jalapeño chillies (or more, to taste), thinly sliced into rings
- salt

Serves 4–6 | Vegetarian

1 Spread a flour tortilla with a thin layer of cream cheese, then sprinkle evenly with a little of the Cheddar and dot some of the chilli rings over it – adding more chillies will increase the heat of the quesadillas. Top with another flour tortilla.

2 Heat a dry frying pan over a medium-high heat, add the quesadilla and cook for 3–4 minutes, until a light golden colour, then turn over and cook for a further 3–4 minutes to colour the other side. Slide on to a chopping board and cut into 6 pieces. Preferably, serve immediately, then assemble and cook the others using the remaining ingredients.

6 Sweet potato chips

- 2 large sweet potatoes, scrubbed and trimmed
- 3 litres (5½ pints) vegetable oil, for deep-frying
- sea salt

Serves 4–6 | Vegetarian

1 Using a sharp knife, cut the sweet potatoes into very thin discs.

2 Heat the vegetable oil in a deep, heavy-based saucepan to 180°C, or until a cube of bread browns in 30 seconds. Fry the sweet potato discs, in batches of 15 or so, for about 4 minutes, until golden brown. Remove with a slotted spoon and place on kitchen paper to absorb excess oil. Keep the cooked crisps hot while you fry the remainder. Lightly sprinkle with sea salt and serve.

7 Chargrilled asparagus

- 600g (1lb 5oz) trimmed asparagus spears
- 1 lime
- 3 tbsp olive oil
- sea salt and pepper

Serves 4–6 | Vegetarian

1 Prepare a charcoal barbecue (see step 2, page 228). Cook the asparagus in a large saucepan of lightly salted boiling water for 4 minutes. Drain, leave to cool, then cut in half lengthways.

2 When the barbecue is nice and hot, arrange the asparagus on the barbecue rack and cook for 5 minutes, turning fairly frequently.

3 Meanwhile, cut the lime in half, squeeze the juice from one half into a large bowl and add the olive oil, a pinch of salt and some pepper. Remove the asparagus from the barbecue, add to the lime juice mixture and mix well. Slice the remaining lime half into thin discs and add these to the bowl. Mix once more and serve warm.

Risotto can lend itself to almost any ingredient in the world. Here are a few examples to show seasonality.

Courgette risotto

- 600g (1lb 5oz) courgettes, chopped
- 2 tbsp finely chopped parsley
- 300g (10½ oz) cooked new potatoes, skinned
- salt and pepper

Basic risotto
- 1.5 litres (2¾ pints) Vegetable stock (*see* page 297)
- 125g (4½ oz) butter
- 4 tbsp light olive oil
- 1 white onion, finely chopped
- 1 head of celery, trimmed and chopped
- 600g (1lb 5oz) Arborio rice
- 200ml (7fl oz) medium-dry white wine
- 100g (3½ oz) Parmesan cheese, grated

Serves 4–6 | Vegetarian

1   First make the risotto. Put the stock into a saucepan, bring it up to a simmer and keep it simmering. Melt half the butter with the olive oil in a heavy-based saucepan, add the onion and celery and fry over a medium heat for 6 minutes, or until soft and translucent, stirring frequently. Add the rice and continue to cook, stirring, for about 8 minutes, until the rice turns almost opaque. Add the wine, stirring continuously, and allow the alcohol to completely evaporate before adding a ladleful of the hot stock. Simmer, stirring, until the stock has been absorbed before adding another ladleful. Continue adding stock in the same way, stirring continuously, until it is all absorbed, about 15 minutes.

2   Add the courgettes and continue to cook, stirring frequently, for 5 minutes, by which time the rice will be tender but with a slight bite; cook for 3 more minutes if you prefer it softer. Add the remaining butter, the parsley and half the Parmesan and stir well. Now season the risotto and serve with the potatoes and the rest of the Parmesan sprinkled on top.

Asparagus risotto

- 600g (1lb 5oz) asparagus, trimmed
- 1 quantity Basic Risotto (*see* above)
- 250ml (9fl oz) prosecco
- 3 tbsp finely chopped chives
- freshly grated Parmesan cheese

Serves 4–6 | Vegetarian

1   Slice the asparagus spears into 4cm (1½in) lengths, retaining the top 5cm (2in) – the sweet tips. Follow steps 1 and 2 of the Courgette risotto method above, using the prosecco in place of the white wine. Then add the asparagus discs and tips instead of the courgette and the chives in place of the parsley. Finish with a sprinkling of Parmesan.

Borlotti bean & radicchio risotto

- 500g (1lb 2oz) fresh borlotti beans, podded weight
- 2 tomatoes
- 6 basil leaves
- 1 garlic clove
- 50ml (2fl oz) red wine vinegar
- 50ml (2fl oz) olive oil
- 1 quantity Basic risotto (*see* above)
- ½ head of radicchio, shredded
- aged balsamic vinegar, for drizzling
- salt and pepper
- freshly grated Parmesan cheese

Serves 4–6 | Vegetarian

1   Put the borlotti beans, tomatoes, basil leaves, garlic clove and red wine vinegar into a saucepan and cover with cold water. Pour in the olive oil and bring to the boil, then reduce the heat and simmer for 1 hour, or until the beans are completely cooked. If the water drops below the level of the beans, top it up with a little hot water. Discard the basil leaves and tomato skins, then spoon 3 tablespoons of the beans into a food processor along with the tomatoes, garlic and all the cooking liquid. Blend until smooth, then return the purée to the remaining whole beans in the pan. Season with salt and pepper and a touch more vinegar, if needed.

2   Add the borlotti mixture to the risotto and continue to cook, stirring frequently, for 5 minutes. Add the radicchio and stir well, by which time the rice will be tender but with a slight bite; cook for 3 more minutes if you prefer it softer. Add the butter and half the Parmesan and stir well. Season and serve with a drizzle of balsamic vinegar, and the rest of the Parmesan sprinkled on top.

Ravioli is a staple dish in Italy and such fun to make. I have filled ravioli with hundreds of different fillings, from mashed potato and white truffle to fresh mozzarella. But one of my favourites is butternut squash, so here it is...

Butternut squash ravioli with brown butter

- 600g (1lb 5oz) butternut squash, peeled and seeds discarded
- 4 tbsp olive oil
- 300g (10¹/₂oz) ricotta cheese
- 150g (5¹/₂oz) Parmesan cheese, finely grated
- whole nutmeg, for grating
- 3 tbsp finely chopped basil
- 1 quantity Pasta dough (*see* page 296)
- 100g (3¹/₂oz) butter
- 1 handful of flat leaf parsley leaves
- salt and pepper

Serves 4–6 | Vegetarian

1   Preheat the oven to 180°C/fan 160°C/gas mark 4. Cut the butternut squash into 6cm (2¹/₂in) cubes. Spread them out on a roasting tray, drizzle with 2 tablespoons of the olive oil and season with salt and pepper. Roast for 30 minutes, or until tender, then remove from the oven and leave to cool. Transfer to a mixing bowl and add the ricotta, half the Parmesan, 10 strokes of nutmeg, the basil, some salt and pepper and the remaining olive oil. Mix together well and set aside at room temperature.

2   Roll out the pasta dough on a lightly floured work surface into a rectangle thin enough to see your hand through, or use a pasta machine set on its widest setting. Cover the pasta that you aren't working on with a clean damp tea towel to prevent it from drying out, folding it back as you work down it in the next step.

3   Place teaspoonfuls of the squash mixture in a line on the dough, spaced about 5cm (2in) apart. Very lightly brush water along the edge and around the small mounds of filling, then fold the pasta over the top and press to join. Press down between the mounds, making sure you push out any air that may have been trapped. Use a fluted pastry wheel or sharp knife to cut the ravioli into any shape you like, but just make sure you have a good seal between the top and bottom sheet.

4   Cook the ravioli in 2 batches in a large saucepan of salted boiling water for 3 minutes, or until they bob back up to the surface. Meanwhile, melt the butter in a saucepan and continue to heat it until it begins to darken a little. Add the parsley, then remove from the heat. Using a slotted spoon transfer the ravioli to serving plates and spoon the brown butter over the top. Finish the dish with the rest of the grated Parmesan and serve immediately.

This is such a comforting soup – the ginger and nutmeg warm you all the way down to your toes. I dropped a nasturtium flower on top of this soup because the colours blended brilliantly.

Butternut squash soup with nutmeg & ginger

- 75ml (2¹/₂fl oz) olive oil
- 1 large white onion, cut into 2cm (³/₄in) cubes
- 1 head of celery, trimmed and cut into 2cm (³/₄in) pieces
- 1kg (2lb 4oz) butternut squash, peeled, deseeded and cut into 2cm (³/₄in) cubes
- 3 garlic cloves, chopped
- 50g (1³/₄oz) fresh root ginger, peeled and cut into tiny cubes
- 1 tsp dried red chilli flakes
- 60g (2¹/₄oz) white long-grain rice
- 200ml (7fl oz) medium-dry white wine
- 1.5 litres (2³/₄ pints) Vegetable stock (*see* page 297)
- whole nutmeg, for grating
- 1 lemon, for squeezing
- salt and pepper
- yellow nasturtium flowers, to garnish (optional)

Serves 4–6 | Vegetarian

1   Heat the olive oil in a large saucepan, add the onion and celery and cook over a medium heat for 5 minutes, stirring occasionally. Add the squash, garlic and ginger, season with salt and pepper then add the chilli flakes. Cook for 15 minutes, stirring occasionally and without allowing the vegetables to catch on the base of the pan too much. Add the rice and cook, stirring, for a further 5 minutes.

2   Stir in the wine and loosen any brown bits stuck to the pan, then allow all the liquid to evaporate before adding the stock. Bring to the boil, then reduce the heat and simmer, uncovered, for 20 minutes, or until the rice is tender. Grate in 10 strokes of nutmeg, add a squeeze of lemon juice and check the seasoning. Pour the soup into bowls and garnish with bright yellow nasturtium flowers, if you can get them.

It's usually devilled kidneys you get on toast, but I like to devil mushrooms. You still get all the flavour, and you can share them with your vegetarian friends too.

Devilled mushrooms on toast

- 50ml (2fl oz) olive oil
- 1kg (2lb 4oz) button mushrooms, wiped and trimmed
- 3 tbsp brandy
- 3 tbsp wholegrain mustard
- 1 tsp paprika
- 200ml (7fl oz) double cream
- juice of 1 lemon
- 6 slices of bread
- 2 tbsp finely chopped flat leaf parsley
- salt and pepper

Serves 3–6 | Vegetarian

1   Heat the olive oil in a frying pan, add the mushrooms and fry over a high heat for 3 minutes. Add the brandy with great care as it may well catch alight as it hits the hot pan, but any flames will quickly die away. Allow the brandy to evaporate, then add the mustard, paprika, cream and lemon juice. Reduce the heat to low and season with salt and pepper.

2   Toast the bread then arrange the slices on serving plates. Add most of the chopped parsley to the mushrooms and stir well. Top the toast with the devilled mushrooms, sprinkle the remaining parsley and serve hot.

Taking the time to cut the mushrooms up rather than using a machine adds a more sophisticated edge to this tasty dish. Get as many wild mushrooms in there as you can for those deep autumnal flavours.

Mushroom duxelle in filo pastry

- 200g (7oz) young girolle mushrooms, wiped and trimmed
- 6 large flat mushrooms, wiped and trimmed
- 100g (3½oz) butter
- 2 large shallots, finely chopped
- 2 garlic cloves, finely chopped
- 2 tbsp finely chopped chives
- 250ml (9fl oz) warm Vegetable stock (*see* page 297)
- 12 sheets of filo pastry
- 2 tbsp olive oil
- 6 tsp crème fraîche
- 1 lemon, for squeezing
- salt and pepper

Serves 4 | Vegetarian

1   Try to choose the smallest girolles for this dish, as it's nice to keep them whole, but if they are bigger than your little finger, pull them in half. Cut the flat mushrooms horizontally at 1cm (½in) intervals, then run the knife along their length to create large matchsticks, and cut these into small dice.

2   Melt half the butter in a large frying pan. When it is bubbling, add the shallots and garlic and fry over a medium heat, stirring, for 2 minutes. Add the mushrooms and cook over a medium-high heat until they give off their liquid and it then evaporates. Now add half the chives, cook for 1 minute, stirring, then pour in the stock. Cook until the stock has reduced to a light coating on the mushrooms. Season with salt and pepper and squeeze in a little lemon juice.

3   Preheat the oven to 180°C/fan 160°C/gas mark 4. Melt the remaining butter in a small saucepan and keep it warm. Lay the first sheet of filo pastry on a work surface and brush very lightly with the melted butter. Lay another sheet of filo on top and again brush very lightly with butter, then repeat the process with a third sheet of filo. Use the entire triple layer of pastry to line a 13cm (5in) ring placed on a baking sheet: this will form a 'basket' to hold the mushroom duxelle. Repeat to make another 3 filo baskets.

4   Bake the filo baskets for 8 minutes until the pastry is a very light golden brown. Remove from the oven, fill with the lovely mushroom mixture, then return to the oven for 4–6 minutes to heat through. Before serving, scatter over the remaining chopped chives and add a teaspoon of crème fraîche to the centre of each basket. Delicious served hot, but really good at room temperature too.

This recipe works out brilliantly with the moistness of the filling and the flavour of the thyme, which really comes through. They kind of look like hamburgers and could be a great alternative – just take out the bacon if you are going fully vegetarian. Serve with a side salad.

Stuffed Portobello mushrooms

- 12 Portobello or any large field mushrooms, wiped and trimmed
- 300g (10½oz) chanterelle mushrooms
- 50g (1¾oz) butter
- 2 large shallots, finely chopped
- 2 garlic cloves, finely chopped
- 8 rashers of streaky bacon, cut into lengths 1cm (½in) wide
- 1 bunch of thyme
- 2 tbsp chopped parsley
- 1 lemon, for squeezing
- 50ml (2fl oz) extra virgin olive oil
- salt and pepper

Serves 4

1   Peel 4 of the Portobello mushrooms, then pull off their stalks and reserve. Carefully spoon out and discard the dark gills and set aside the caps to await filling. Trim the reserved stalks and finely chop. Peel the remaining Portobello mushrooms and trim the stalks. Set 4 aside to be used as lids, then chop the remainder fairly finely and combine with the other gills and chopped stalks. Split any large chanterelles in half and add to the chopped mushrooms.

2   Preheat the oven to 180°C/fan 160°C/gas mark 4. Melt the butter in a large frying pan, and just as it begins to foam add the shallots and garlic, then stir in the bacon and cook over a medium heat for 5 minutes, stirring frequently. Add the chopped mushrooms to the pan and fry for a further 6 minutes. Pick the leaves from half the bunch of thyme, add to the pan and season with salt and pepper, then add the parsley and squeeze in a little lemon juice. Turn off the heat.

3   Set the Portobello caps for filling, cavity-side up, on a roasting tray. Fill with the cooked mushrooms and cover with the reserved mushroom lids. You will then have what look like mushroom burgers. Push a large wooden cocktail stick through each to secure. Drizzle the olive oil all over the mushrooms, scatter over the remaining thyme sprigs and season with salt and pepper. Roast for 20 minutes. Serve warm.

This salad is so delicate and the flavours work totally harmoniously. If you ever have porcini to hand, you absolutely must try this recipe.

Raw porcini salad with Parmesan & parsley

- 800g (1lb 12oz) porcini mushrooms, brushed and trimmed
- 200g (7oz) Parmesan cheese
- 1 handful of flat leaf parsley
- 75ml (2½fl oz) extra virgin olive oil
- 1 lemon, for squeezing
- sea salt

Serves 4–6 | Vegetarian

1   Cut the mushrooms into slices 1cm (½in) thick and arrange them on serving plates.

2   Cut or shave the Parmesan super thinly and sprinkle it over the mushrooms. Now cut the parsley into very thin strips, sprinkle this over each plate, then drizzle with olive oil. Add a squeeze of lemon juice, keeping it to a minimum or it will kill the other flavours (just a touch of lemon juice in the right place can really make a dish sing). Finish the plates with a sprinkling of sea salt and serve quickly.

Using a pasta machine can be very helpful, but when I was learning my trade in Italy, the real masters turned up their noses at pasta machines in favour of wooden rolling pins and boards. They said they could taste metal in the pasta when prepared on a machine. And you know what? Pasta rolled out with a rolling pin does have a slightly softer feel to it.

Handmade tagliatelle with porcini & girolles

- 800g (1lb 12oz) porcini mushrooms, brushed and trimmed
- 400g (14oz) girolle mushrooms, wiped and trimmed
- 75g (2¾oz) butter
- 2 large shallots, finely chopped
- 2 garlic cloves, finely chopped
- 150ml (¼ pint) medium-dry white wine
- 200ml (7fl oz) Vegetable stock (*see* page 297)
- 100ml (3½fl oz) double cream
- 1 quantity Pasta dough (*see* page 296)
- 3 tbsp chopped flat leaf parsley
- salt and pepper
- freshly grated Parmesan cheese, to serve

Serves 4–6 | Vegetarian

1   Melt the butter in a large frying pan, add the shallots and garlic and cook over a medium heat for about 6 minutes until soft, stirring frequently. Add the mushrooms and cook over a medium heat until they have released their liquid and it has then evaporated.

2   Stir the wine into the pan to loosen any brown bits stuck to the base, then allow all the liquid to evaporate before adding the stock. Continue to cook until the stock has reduced by half. Season with salt and pepper and add the cream, then reduce the heat to the lowest setting while you prepare the tagliatelle.

3   Weigh out 200g (7oz) of the pasta dough (keep the rest wrapped in clingfilm). Place it on a lightly floured surface and roll into a rectangle thin enough that you can see your hand through the pasta. Cut the pasta sheet into long strips about 3cm (1¼in) wide using a knife or a fluted pastry wheel to give the dish added character. Repeat the process with the remaining pasta dough.

4   Cook the tagliatelle in a large saucepan of salted boiling water for 2 minutes, or until it floats to the surface. While the pasta is cooking, add the parsley to the warm mushroom sauce. Drain the pasta and add to the sauce. Toss the whole mixture well but don't stir it, as I find that it breaks up the delicate pasta. Lift the tagliatelle on to serving plates and grate a little Parmesan over the top. Serve straight away.

Polenta takes an age to make – well, at least 50 minutes – and if you're going to grill it, you have to let it cool so that it firms up enough to cut. Grilled polenta is perfect for using up the leftover soft polenta from the day before. This is why I always make more soft polenta than I need.

Creamed girolles with grilled polenta

- **800ml (1¹/₃ pints) cold water**
- **400g (14oz) polenta**
- **50g (1³/₄oz) butter**
- **2 large shallots, finely chopped**
- **2 garlic cloves, finely chopped**
- **1kg (2lb 4oz) girolle mushrooms, wiped and trimmed**
- **250ml (9fl oz) Vegetable stock (*see* page 297)**
- **250ml (9fl oz) double cream**
- **3 tbsp chopped flat leaf parsley, plus extra sprigs to garnish**
- **salt and pepper**

Serves 4–6 | Vegetarian

1   If you are preparing the polenta from scratch, start this part of the dish in the morning before serving in the evening. Bring the water to the boil in a large saucepan and season with a pinch of salt. As it comes to the boil, slowly pour in the polenta, whisking constantly with a balloon whisk. The mixture will slowly thicken, and as it begins to bubble like lava, stop adding the polenta and swap your whisk for a wooden spoon. Reduce the heat to low and leave to cook, stirring occasionally, until it begins to pull away from the side of the pan as you stir – about 40–50 minutes. Just make sure it doesn't stick to the bottom.

2   Pour the polenta on to a large plate and leave it to cool completely until firm – placing it in the refrigerator for an hour is a good idea to really firm it up.

3   Melt the butter in a frying pan, add the shallots and garlic and cook over a medium heat for about 6 minutes, until soft, stirring frequently. Add the mushrooms and cook over a medium heat until they have released their liquid and it has then evaporated. Add the stock, stirring, to loosen any brown bits stuck to the pan, then allow it to reduce by half. Season with salt and pepper, add the cream and half the chopped parsley, then reduce the heat to low and keep warm.

4   Preheat the grill to high. Cut the polenta into slices, making each different slice a shape, which I think adds a bit of drama to your plate. Lay the polenta slices on the grill rack and cook until a nice dark brown, lightly charred colour. Transfer to serving plates, spoon the warm mushroom sauce over the top and scatter over the remaining chopped parsley. Garnish with parsley sprigs and serve straight away.

The autumn bounty serves up so many mushrooms that eating all of them can be difficult, so preserve them under oil and come back to them whenever you want. You can use this recipe for most wild mushrooms. Broad beans, which are abundant in spring, can be treated the same way. Try as I might to keep these preserves stored away, they are always swiftly eaten.

Girolles under oil

- 500g (1lb 2oz) girolle mushrooms, wiped and trimmed
- 300ml (1½ pint) olive oil
- 2 large shallots, finely chopped
- 1 garlic clove, finely chopped
- 2 tsp thyme leaves
- 3 tbsp medium-dry white wine
- 150ml (½ pint) Vegetable stock (*see* page 297)
- salt and pepper

Makes 1 small (500ml) jar
Vegetarian

1   Roughly chop the mushrooms. Heat 2 tablespoons olive oil in a frying pan, add the shallots and garlic and cook over a medium heat for about 6 minutes, until soft, stirring frequently. Add the mushrooms and cook over a high heat until they have released their liquid and it has then evaporated. Stir in the thyme leaves.

2   Stir the wine into the pan to loosen any brown bits stuck to the base, then allow all the liquid to evaporate before adding the stock. Continue to cook until the stock is just a sticky residue. Season with salt and pepper. Leave to cool completely.

3   Sterilize a small Kilner-type glass jar, following step 3 of the method on page 180. Spoon the mushroom mixture into the sterilized jar. Pour in the remaining olive oil, making sure that everything is fully covered, then seal. Store in a cool, dark place, but not in the refrigerator, or the olive oil will go cloudy. Use within 2 months. Once opened, refrigerate and use within 2 weeks.

Broad beans under oil with shallots

- 500g (1lb 2oz) broad beans, podded weight
- 300ml (½ pint) olive oil
- 1 tsp fennel seeds
- 2 shallots, finely chopped
- 1 lemon, for squeezing
- salt and pepper

Makes 1 small (500 ml) jar
Vegetarian

1   Cook the broad beans in a saucepan of salted boiling water for 4 minutes. Drain and refresh them in cold water, then drain again. Peel off the skins then set the beans aside at room temperature.

2   Heat 50ml (2fl oz) of the olive oil in a saucepan, add the fennel seeds and fry over a medium heat until they begin to pop. Add the shallots and cook for about 5 minutes, until soft, stirring frequently, then add the peeled beans and a tiny squeeze of lemon juice. Mix well and leave to cool completely.

3   Follow step 3 of the method above to finish and store.

Lentil
Black-eyed pea
Chickpea
Butterbean
Broad bean
Borlotti bean
Pea
Sugarsnap
Mangetout
Runner bean
French bean
Okra

Beans & Pods

This is such a creamy salad. I love goats' cheese, and when it's combined with sun-dried tomatoes, all kinds of crazy flavours kick off. The Baby Gem lettuce gives the salad structure, and pulling this out at a picnic will make you the envy of the other picnickers.

Puy lentil salad with goats' cheese & sun-dried tomatoes

- 400g (14oz) dried Puy lentils
- 6 heads of Baby Gem lettuce
- 100g (3½oz) sun-dried tomatoes in oil, drained
- 200g (7oz) goats' cheese
- 4 tbsp House dressing (*see* page 297)
- 4 tbsp olive oil
- salt and pepper

Serves 4–6 | Vegetarian

1   Rinse the lentils under cold running water. Put them into a saucepan and cover with fresh cold water by a depth of about 5cm (2in). Bring to the boil, then reduce the heat and simmer for 25–30 minutes, until just tender but still with some bite – it's better for the salad if they are al dente rather than soft. Drain the lentils and set aside.

2   Shred the lettuce and put it into a mixing bowl. Slice the sun-dried tomatoes into matchsticks and add them to the bowl. Crumble in chunks of the goats' cheese then add the lentils. Drizzle in the dressing and delicately mix the salad together with your fingertips. Season with salt and pepper and arrange the salad on serving plates. Lightly sprinkle the olive oil over the top and serve.

I served this for years on my menus in Spain, using organic vegetables and making it fresh every day, so people just kept coming back for more. It's had a long history already, so I'm pleased to be able to pass it on to you.

Lentil tart with sweet potato & crème fraîche

- 300g (10¹/₂oz) cooked and drained Puy lentils
- 2 tbsp Dijon mustard
- butter, for greasing
- plain flour, for dusting
- 500g (1lb 2oz) Shortcrust Pastry (*see* page 296)
- 300g (10¹/₂oz) Swiss chard, cut into 5cm (2in) pieces
- 75ml (2¹/₂fl oz) olive oil
- 1 large red onion, finely chopped
- 2 garlic cloves, finely chopped
- 300g (10¹/₂oz) sweet potato, cut into 2cm (³/₄in) cubes
- 6 tbsp crème fraîche
- 3 tbsp finely chopped flat leaf parsley
- 100g (3¹/₂oz) soft white breadcrumbs
- salt and pepper

Serves 4–6 | Vegetarian

1   Make sure the lentils are soft to the bite – it helps to structure the tart if they are a little soft. Season with salt, pepper and the mustard and set aside.

2   Grease a 26cm (10¹/₂in) pastry ring 8cm (3¹/₄in) deep and dust with flour. Place it on a baking sheet lined with greaseproof paper. Roll out the pastry on a lightly floured work surface and use to line the ring. Leave to rest in the refrigerator for 30 minutes.

3   Meanwhile, cook the Swiss chard in a saucepan of salted boiling water for 5 minutes, then drain and set aside. Heat half the olive oil in a frying pan, add the onion and garlic and cook over a medium heat for 5 minutes, until the onion is soft, stirring frequently. Add the chard, season with salt and pepper and slowly braise the chard mixture for 10 minutes, stirring occasionally. Meanwhile, cook the sweet potatoes in a saucepan of salted boiling water for 25 minutes, until they are just tender but still with a slight bite. Drain and set aside. Preheat the oven to 180°C/fan 160°C/gas mark 4.

4   Line the chilled pastry case with greaseproof paper, fill with dried beans and bake for 15 minutes. Lift out the paper and beans and leave the pastry case to cool. Mix the chard, lentils and sweet potato with 2 tablespoons of the crème fraîche. Check the seasoning and add half the parsley. Mix well and spoon the mixture into the pastry case. Sprinkle the breadcrumbs and the rest of the parsley over the tart, drizzle over the remaining olive oil, then return to the oven for 15–20 minutes to colour the top and heat the middle. Serve in slices with dollops of the remaining crème fraîche on the side.

The first time I cooked this dish I pulled the leftovers out of the fridge the following day and had them for lunch. Wow! The flavours were fantastic, even when cold. The pickled chillies really wake up the taste buds.

Black-eyed peas with ham hock & pickled chillies

- 1 ham hock, soaked in cold water overnight and drained
- 400g (14oz) dried black-eyed peas, soaked in cold water overnight
- 4 bay leaves
- 2 small white onions
- 3 tbsp Dijon mustard
- 2 garlic cloves, peeled but left whole
- 2 bunches of young carrots, scrubbed and leaves trimmed
- 6 small pickled red chillies, trimmed and cut into short lengths
- salt and pepper

Serves 4–6

1   Put the ham hock into a saucepan large enough to cover it with water by a depth of 10cm (4in). Bring to the boil, then drain and return to the pan with the black-eyed beans, bay leaves, onions, mustard and garlic cloves, cover with cold water and bring to the boil. Reduce the heat and simmer for 1 3/4 hours, skimming off any white foam that rises to the surface.

2   Add the carrots and pickled chillies and cook for a further 25 minutes, then season with salt and pepper. The hock is ready when you can scoop it from the bone with a spoon. Pour away most of the cooking liquid, but retain a little, as you may like to keep the leftovers in the liquid. Slice the ham, and serve with the beans and vegetables alongside. This dish is great served cold too.

This dish is the type of cooking I do every day at home. All the ingredients complement each other brilliantly, are super-nutritious and can be eaten as a complete meal.

Braised chickpeas with chard, fennel & tomato

- 400g (14oz) dried chickpeas, soaked in cold water overnight and drained
- 400g (14oz) red chard, cut into 2cm (3/4in) pieces
- 2 fennel bulbs, trimmed and tough outer leaves discarded
- 75ml (2¹/2fl oz) olive oil
- 2 garlic cloves, thinly sliced
- 2 tsp fennel seeds
- 1 tsp dried red chilli flakes
- 2 red onions, finely diced
- 2 tomatoes, roughly chopped
- 2 tbsp herb vinegar

Serves 4–6 | Vegetarian

1   Put the chickpeas into a large saucepan and cover well with fresh cold water. Bring to the boil, skimming off any white foam that rises to the surface, then reduce the heat and simmer for 1 hour, or until just tender but still with some bite. Drain and set aside.

2   Meanwhile, cook the chard in a saucepan of salted boiling water for 5 minutes, then drain and set aside. Cut each fennel bulb into eighths and cook in a separate saucepan of salted boiling water for 5 minutes, then drain and set aside.

3   Heat the olive oil in a saucepan. Add the garlic, fennel seeds and chilli flakes and cook over a medium heat for 2 minutes, until the garlic starts to turn golden brown, stirring occasionally. Add the onions and cook for 5 minutes, again stirring occasionally. Add the tomatoes and chickpeas and cook for another 5 minutes before adding the cooked chard and fennel and the vinegar. Stir through, season with salt and pepper and serve.

Blackening onions creates a wonderful flavour and keeps them slightly crunchy, which is reminiscent of Turkish cooking. The smoky paprika really pushes the taste buds too.

Chickpea stew with grilled onions & smoked paprika

- 400g (14oz) dried chickpeas, soaked in cold water overnight and drained
- 2 tbsp olive oil, plus extra for sprinkling
- 2 garlic cloves, thinly sliced
- 1 tsp dried chilli flakes
- 3 bay leaves
- 4 tbsp finely chopped white onion
- 2 large white Spanish onions, cut through the root into 8 sections
- 2 tbsp white wine vinegar
- smoked paprika, for dusting
- salt and pepper

Serves 4–6 | Vegetarian

1   Put the chickpeas into a large saucepan and cover well with fresh cold water. Bring to the boil, skimming off any white foam that rises to the surface, then reduce the heat and simmer for 1 hour, or until just tender but still with some bite. Drain and set aside.

2   Meanwhile, heat the olive oil in a large saucepan. Add the garlic and bay leaves and cook over a medium heat for about 2 minutes, until the garlic starts to turn a golden brown, stirring occasionally. Add the chopped onion and cook for 5 minutes, again stirring occasionally. Add the chickpeas and cook for another 5 minutes, then season with salt and pepper.

3   Preheat the grill to medium-high. Arrange the onion sections on a roasting tray so they are sitting on their curved side. Sprinkle them with the vinegar and some olive oil and place them under the grill for about 6 minutes, until the tops turn dark brown, even lightly charred.

4   Arrange the onions on a serving plate with their juices, then spoon the chickpea mixture around them. Lightly dust smoked paprika over the top of the whole dish and serve straight away.

Feast: Curry

I recently had one of the best culinary experiences of my life. An elderly Bengali chef came into my kitchen and cooked with me for a week – creamy dahls, wicked curries and simple potato dishes. It inspired me to come up with loads of new ideas for taking vegetables in different directions. So here's a vegetarian feast that you simply won't be able to stop eating. The Butter bean & mango curry uses turmeric and ginger to push your taste buds. You may be a little surprised at the use of salsify in a curry, but try it – it's incredible! Yam & coconut go brilliantly together here, the Sag aloo is the best recipe ever and the Lentil dahl with cinnamon & Indian bay is like no other. Green bean & spicy chapattis are delicious and so easy to make. Serve with mango chutney, yoghurt, boiled rice and plain chapattis.

Curry

1 Butter bean & mango curry

- 50g (1³⁄₄oz) butter
- 50ml (2fl oz) olive oil
- ½ tsp cumin seeds
- 1 large white onion, chopped
- 1 small garlic clove, finely chopped
- 1 tsp turmeric
- 1 tsp garam masala
- 1 tsp peeled and grated fresh root ginger
- ½ tsp dried red chilli flakes
- 2 tomatoes, roughly chopped
- 250g (9oz) cooked butter beans
- 1 mango, peeled, stoned and cut into 2–3cm (³⁄₄in–1¹⁄₄in) cubes
- salt and pepper

Serves 4–6 | Vegetarian

1 Melt the butter with the olive oil in a saucepan. Add the cumin seeds and heat over a medium-high heat until the butter foams, then add the onion and garlic and cook for 5 minutes, until the onion is slightly coloured, stirring occasionally.

2 Add the turmeric, garam masala, ginger and chilli flakes to the pan and cook for 4 minutes, stirring frequently, then add the tomatoes and cook for 5 minutes, stirring occasionally. Stir in the butter beans and mango, season with salt and pepper and add a touch of water to the dish if it seems a little dry. Heat through and serve hot.

2 Curried salsify with coriander

- 50g (1³⁄₄oz) butter
- 2 tbsp vegetable oil
- 1 fresh hot green chilli, deseeded and finely chopped
- 2cm (³⁄₄in) piece of fresh root ginger, peeled and finely chopped
- 1 tsp cumin seeds
- ½ tsp black mustard seeds
- 6 large salsify, peeled and cut into 7 x 2cm (2³⁄₄ x ³⁄₄in) pieces
- 2 large tomatoes, roughly chopped
- 2 tsp ground coriander
- ½ tsp turmeric
- ½ tsp garam masala
- 1 tsp soft light brown sugar
- ½ tsp salt
- 3 tbsp chopped coriander
- 2–3 tsp lemon juice

Serves 4–6 | Vegetarian

1 Heat the butter with the vegetable oil in a saucepan. Add the chilli, ginger, cumin and mustard seeds and fry over a medium-high heat until the seeds begin to pop and crack, stirring frequently. Add the salsify and cook for 5 minutes.

2 Add the tomatoes to the pan with the ground coriander, turmeric, garam masala, sugar, salt and half the coriander. Cook over a medium heat

for 20 minutes, or until the salsify is soft to the knife but not mushy, stirring occasionally. Check the seasoning, add the remaining coriander, the lemon juice to taste and serve hot.

3 Yam & coconut curry

- 50ml (2fl oz) vegetable oil
- 1 tsp cumin seeds
- 1 large white onion, finely chopped
- 1 garlic clove, finely chopped
- 1 fresh red chilli, finely chopped
- 2 yams, cut into 2cm (³⁄₄in) cubes
- 400ml (14fl oz) hot Vegetable stock (see page 297)
- 200ml (7fl oz) coconut milk
- 2–3 tsp lime juice
- 3 tbsp chopped coriander
- salt and pepper

Serves 4–6 | Vegetarian

1 Heat the vegetable oil in a saucepan, add the cumin seeds and fry over a medium-high heat until they begin to pop and crack, stirring frequently. Add the onion and garlic and cook until they are soft but not coloured, stirring frequently, then add the chilli and yam and cook for 5 minutes, stirring occasionally.

2 Pour in the hot stock, bring to the boil and cook until reduced by two-thirds, stirring frequently, about 20 minutes. Add the coconut milk and return the curry to the boil, then reduce the heat to low. Season, add the lime juice and coriander and cook for a further 2 minutes before serving.

4 Sag aloo

- 100g (3½oz) butter
- 50ml (2fl oz) olive oil
- ½ tsp cumin seeds
- 1 large white onion, chopped
- 1 small garlic clove, finely chopped
- 1 tsp turmeric
- 1 tsp garam masala
- 1 tsp peeled and grated fresh root ginger
- 400g (14oz) spinach, roughly chopped
- 12 small floury potatoes, scrubbed and cooked whole
- salt and pepper

Serves 4–6 | Vegetarian

1 Melt the butter with the olive oil in a saucepan. Add the cumin seeds and fry over a medium-high heat until the butter foams, then add the onion and garlic and cook for 5 minutes, until the onion is slightly coloured, stirring occasionally.

2 Add the turmeric, garam masala and ginger to the pan and cook for 4 minutes, stirring frequently. Add the spinach and let it wilt, then cook for 5 minutes, stirring occasionally. Stir in the cooked potatoes, season with salt and pepper and add a touch of water to the dish if it seems a little dry. Heat through and serve hot.

5 Lentil dahl with cinnamon & Indian bay

- 600g (1lb 5oz) dried red lentils
- 4 Indian bay leaves
- 1 cinnamon stick
- 1 tsp cumin seeds
- 1 tsp dried red chilli flakes
- 3 tbsp vegetable oil
- 8 garlic cloves, thinly sliced
- salt and pepper

Serves 4–6 | Vegetarian

1 Drain the lentils and rinse them in several changes of cold water, until the water runs clean. Put the lentils into a saucepan and cover with fresh cold water by a depth of 7cm (2³⁄₄in). Add the bay leaves, cinnamon, cumin and chilli flakes and bring to the boil.

2 Heat the vegetable oil in a frying pan, add the garlic and fry over a medium heat for 4–5 minutes, stirring occasionally and watching carefully, until the garlic is light golden brown all over – the secret to dahl. Just as the garlic reaches this desired golden state, tip the whole contents of the frying pan into the lentils, which will cough and splutter for a second or so but then calm down. Reduce the heat and simmer for 25 minutes, or until the lentils are tender and liquid absorbed – the consistency should be runny porridge. Season with salt and pepper and serve hot.

6 Green bean & spicy carrot chapattis

- 300g (10½oz) French beans
- 300g (10½oz) carrot, cut into batons
- 50g (1³⁄₄oz) butter
- 3 tbsp olive oil
- 1 small white onion, finely chopped
- 1 garlic clove, finely chopped
- 2 tsp curry powder
- 2 tomatoes, chopped
- 2 tsp lemon juice
- 6 chapatti

Serves 3–6 | Vegetarian

1 Put the french beans and carrot batons in a pan of fresh cold water, bring to the boil and cook for 4 minutes or until al dente. Drain and reserve. Preheat the oven to 180°C/fan 160°C/gas mark 4.

2 Melt the butter with the olive oil in a saucepan. Add the onion and garlic and cook for 5–7minutes until soft. Add the curry powder and fry for 5 minutes more. Add the chopped tomatoes and lemon juice and cook for 10 minutes. Add the carrots and beans and stir to coat with the sauce. Lay the chapattis onto a clean flat surface and spoon the bean mixture into the centre of each. Roll into cigar shapes, and place on a roasting tray. Warm for 3 minutes before serving.

My kids love stuffing pitta bread with all kinds of things, and this recipe captures the best of the stuffings. Just cut out the chilli if serving to little ones.

Falafel, pitta bread & cucumber salsa

- 250g (9oz) cooked chickpeas
- 1 large white onion, finely chopped
- 2 garlic cloves, finely chopped
- 3 tbsp finely chopped flat leaf parsley
- 1 tsp ground coriander
- 1 tsp tahini
- 1 tsp ground cumin
- 2 tbsp chickpea (gram) flour,
  or plain flour if unavailable
- light olive oil, for deep-frying
- 6 pitta breads
- salt and pepper

Cucumber salsa
- 200g (7oz) cucumber
- 200g (7oz) tomato
- 1 fresh red chilli, deseeded and chopped
- 2 tbsp chopped mint
- 2 tbsp chopped coriander
- juice of 1/2 lemon
- 50ml (2fl oz) olive oil
- salt and pepper

Serves 6 | Vegetarian

1   For the salsa, cut the cucumber and tomato into small dice and place in a mixing bowl. Add the chilli, mint and coriander to the bowl. Squeeze in the lemon juice, drizzle in the olive oil and season with salt and pepper. Mix well and set aside.

2   Put the chickpeas in a food processor with all the other ingredients except the oil and pitta breads. Blend to a thick paste.

3   Roll a tablespoonful of the paste into a ball between your palms and then press it slightly flat. Repeat with the remaining paste until it is all used up – you should have 12 falafel.

4   Heat a 7.5cm (3in) depth of light olive oil in a deep, heavy-based saucepan to 180°C, or until a cube of bread browns in 30 seconds. Fry the falafels in 2 or 3 batches for about 3–5 minutes, until they are golden brown. Remove with a slotted spoon and drain on kitchen paper. Keep the cooked falafel warm while you fry the remainder.

5   Warm the pitta breads in a toaster, not allowing them to become too crunchy. Cut them in half horizontally and tuck a falafel into each cavity. Top with the tangy salsa and serve straight away.

Most of the best cooking relies on classic combinations and flavour relationships, and in this recipe the tarragon, mustard and vinegar make one of those combinations. I've just added the beans and lentils.

Butterbean salad with tarragon & mustard

- **500g (1lb 2oz) dried butterbeans, soaked in cold water overnight**
- **200g (7oz) cooked Puy lentils**
- **2 shallots, finely chopped**
- **2 tbsp finely chopped tarragon**
- **2 tbsp Dijon mustard**
- **75ml (2¹/₂fl oz) olive oil**
- **2 tbsp white wine vinegar**
- **salt and pepper**

Serves 4–6 | Vegetarian

1   Drain the butterbeans, put them into a large saucepan and cover well with fresh cold water. Bring to the boil and boil rapidly for 10 minutes, skimming off any white foam that rises to the surface. Reduce the heat and simmer for 45 minutes, or until tender.

2   Drain the beans in a colander and transfer to a mixing bowl. While still warm, add all the other ingredients, mix well and season with salt and pepper. Serve warm.

These two dishes are great with cold beer, and can really add to a table of tapas or snacks. Serve them alongside peanuts and crisps for a party, or just bag them up and take them with you on a journey.

Spiced crunchy butterbeans

– 500g (1lb 2oz) butter beans
– 3 litres (5¼ pints) sunflower oil, for deep-frying
– 4 tbsp hot paprika
– 1 tbsp icing sugar
– 1 tbsp fine salt

Serves 4–6 | **Vegetarian**

1   Blanch the butterbeans in a saucepan of boiling water for 2 minutes, then drain and refresh them in cold water. Heat the sunflower oil in a deep, heavy-based saucepan to 180°C, or until a cube of bread browns in 30 seconds. Meanwhile peel the beans, then split them in half along their natural divide.

2   Fry the beans in batches for 4 minutes, or until they are golden and crunchy. Remove each batch of beans with a slotted spoon and drain on kitchen paper.

3   Mix the paprika with the icing sugar and salt and dust this mixture over the hot fried beans before serving.

Broad bean & polenta chips

– 3 litres (5¼ pints) sunflower oil, for deep-frying
– 1 quantity cooked polenta (*see* steps 1 and 2, page 250)
– 400g (14oz) broad beans, podded weight
– 4 tbsp hot paprika
– 1 tbsp icing sugar
– 1 tbsp fine salt

Serves 4–6 | **Vegetarian**

1   Gently tear the polenta into roughly equal pieces, of different shapes. Heat the sunflower oil and blanch, drain and refresh the broad beans then peel and split them as in step 1 above.

2   Fry and drain the beans, in batches, as in step 2 above. Fry and drain the polenta in the same way.

3   Mix the paprika with the icing sugar and salt as above and dust over the hot fried beans and polenta. Serve immediately.

When I was first shown this recipe by Rose Gray at the River Café in London, I couldn't believe how simple it was, and that it had made it onto the menu. Years later, every time I see a young broad bean I still hanker to make this smashed recipe. In fact, if you are a young broad bean, watch out!

Smashed broad beans with pecorino

- 1 garlic clove
- 2 tsp sea salt
- 10 mint leaves
- 500g (1lb 2oz) very young broad beans, podded weight
- 100ml (3½fl oz) extra virgin olive oil, plus extra for drizzling
- 150g (5½oz) pecorino cheese, freshly grated
- 1 tsp lemon juice
- 6 slices of bread

Serves 4–6 | Vegetarian

1   Put the garlic into a large mortar with 1 teaspoon of the sea salt and pound with a pestle to a fine paste. Add the mint leaves and pound again into a paste. Add a handful of the broad beans and pound to a fine paste, then add a further handful and pound again. Continue adding and pounding the remaining beans in the same way. It will become increasingly difficult to make a paste as you add more beans, but this creates the desired chunky texture of the dish.

2   Add the olive oil and mix well, then add the pecorino with the remaining teaspoon of salt and the lemon juice. Transfer to a serving bowl.

3   Toast the bread slices and cut in half diagonally. Serve alongside the bowl of smashed beans with some extra olive oil for drizzling.

Tinned beans on toast is probably one of my favourite comfort foods. I can certainly remember growing up on them – and loving them. I like this recipe because it's a grown-up version of that simple dish.

Baked borlotti beans on toast

- **500g (1lb 2oz) borlotti beans, podded weight**
- **2 tomatoes, roughly chopped**
- **6 sage leaves**
- **1 garlic clove**
- **50ml (2fl oz) spiced white wine vinegar, plus extra if needed and for dressing the rocket**
- **50ml (2fl oz) olive oil, plus extra for dressing the rocket**
- **4 slices of bread**
- **1 bunch of wild rocket**
- **butter, for spreading**
- **salt and pepper**

Serves 4 | Vegetarian

1 Put the borlotti beans, tomatoes, sage leaves, garlic clove and vinegar into a large saucepan and cover with cold water. Pour in the olive oil and bring to the boil, then reduce the heat and simmer for 1 hour, or until the beans are completely cooked. If the water drops below the level of the beans, top it up with a little hot water.

2 Remove and discard the sage leaves and tomato skins, then spoon 3 tablespoons of the beans into a food processor along with the tomatoes, garlic and all the cooking liquid. Blend until smooth, then return the purée to the remaining whole beans in the pan. Season with salt and pepper and – if it needs it – a touch more vinegar.

3 Toast your bread. Meanwhile, lightly dress the rocket with a little olive oil and spiced vinegar. Gently squeeze with your hands to bruise the leaves. Butter the toast, put on plates and spoon over the seasoned beans. Garnish with the dressed rocket.

This is a play on one of my favourite Japanese snacks, edamame or soya beans. All I have done is swap fresh young soya beans in their pods for garden peas in their pods, and it really works. If you can get it try fleur de sel, the briny French sea salt that is slightly moist and packed full of minerals – it really sticks to the pods well.

Steamed peas in their pods with salt & olive oil

- **3 tbsp sea salt, or fleur de sel**
- **olive oil, for drizzling**
- **1kg (2lb 4oz) young garden peas in their pods**

Serves 4 | Vegetarian

1   Bring a large saucepan of water to the boil and add 1 tablespoon of the salt. Add the peas in their pods and boil for 3 minutes.

2   Drain in a colander, return to the pan and drizzle with olive oil, stirring to coat the peas. Serve immediately, sprinkled with the remaining salt.

Grilled broad beans in their pods

Heat a barbecue (*see* step 1, page 228) or a griddle pan and, when hot, place 1kg (2lb 4oz) of whole broad bean pods on to the grill. Cook until charred and turn once, to cook the beans to perfection. Remove from the heat, pod the beans and serve with olive oil and a good squeeze of lemon juice.

This is liked big time by my kids. If you want to spice the whole affair up for adults, add some Worcestershire sauce, Tabasco and a little crushed garlic to the pea mixture.

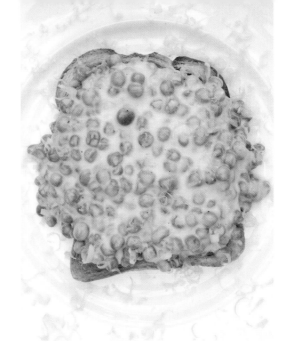

Cheesy peas on toast

- 50g (1³/₄oz) butter, plus extra for buttering the toast
- 50g (1³/₄oz) plain flour
- 500ml (18fl oz) milk, warmed, plus extra if needed
- whole nutmeg, for grating
- 250g (9oz) Cheddar cheese, grated
- 50g (1³/₄oz) Parmesan cheese, freshly grated
- 500g (1lb 2oz) fresh or frozen peas, podded weight
- 4 slices of bread
- salt and pepper

Serves 4 | Vegetarian

1   Melt the butter in a saucepan until it foams. Turn down the heat, mix in the flour and cook gently, stirring for 4–5 minutes without allowing the roux to colour. With the pan still on the heat, slowly whisk in the milk, then increase the heat, bring to the boil and cook until thickened, whisking well to avoid lumps. Season lightly with salt, pepper and nutmeg, then stir in the Cheddar followed by the Parmesan. Keep the sauce warm.

2   Cook the peas in a saucepan of salted boiling water for 5 minutes. Drain then add to the cheese sauce and mix well. Toast your bread, butter it and arrange on serving plates. If the cheesy peas are not wet enough to pour over the toast, add a little more milk and stir well. Spoon the peas over the toast and serve.

Serve these lollies on a hot day as an afternoon snack. You can make them any shape you like: even putting the mixture into an ice cube tray and inserting wooden ice lolly sticks would work a treat.

Iced pea & mint lollipops

- **500g (1lb 2oz) freshly picked young peas, podded weight**
- **50g (1³/₄oz) butter**
- **2 shallots, finely diced**
- **1 tbsp caster sugar**
- **150ml (¼ pint) double cream**
- **2 tbsp finely chopped mint leaves**
- **salt and pepper**

Makes 6 large lollies or 12 small ones | Vegetarian

1 Cook the peas in a saucepan of salted boiling water for 3 minutes, then drain.

2 Melt the butter in a saucepan, add the shallots and cook gently for 4 minutes, stirring frequently. Add the peas, mix together, then season with the sugar, salt and pepper. Add the cream and bring to the boil briefly, before reducing the heat and adding the mint.

3 Leave to cool for a few minutes, then transfer to a to a blender and blend until almost smooth, but with some small chunks of pea. Spoon the mixture into ice-lolly moulds and freeze until firm.

This recipe always works wonders for me in the summer. Sipping a cooling soup at home in the garden always kick-starts the senses. A nice bottle of white wine goes down really well with this dish too.

Chilled pea soup with lemon thyme

- 50g (1¾oz) butter
- 1 large white onion, finely chopped
- 2 small potatoes, finely chopped
- 200ml (7fl oz) medium-dry white wine
- 500g (1lb 2oz) fresh or frozen peas, podded weight
- 1 litre (1¾ pints) hot Vegetable stock (*see* page 297)
- 250ml (9fl oz) double cream
- 2 tbsp lemon thyme leaves
- salt and pepper

Serves 4–6 | Vegetarian

1   Melt the butter in a saucepan, add the onion and cook over a medium heat for 5 minutes without colouring, stirring frequently. Add the potato and cook for 7 minutes, stirring occasionally.

2   Add the wine to the pan and cook until all the liquid has evaporated. Add the peas and stir well, pour in the hot stock and bring to a simmer. Cook for 8 minutes, or until the potatoes are soft.

3   Leave to cool for a few minutes, then transfer to a blender in batches and blend until smooth, adding the cream as you do so, plus half the lemon thyme leaves and some seasoning. Pour the soup into a mixing bowl and leave to cool completely before covering with clingfilm and refrigerating for at least 2 hours. Serve the soup cold, sprinkled with the rest of the thyme leaves.

Sometimes the simple dishes surprise you the most, and these are two of them. The little trick of cooking the chilli flakes with the peas in the boiling water is a nice one and can be used in other dishes. I love the crunch of sugarsnap peas – they really excite the palate and lend themselves to all types of dishes. Keeping them simple, fresh and crunchy is the best way to eat them.

Buttered peas with lettuce & chilli

- 500g (1lb 2oz) fresh or frozen peas, podded weight
- 1 pinch of dried red chilli flakes
- 4 heads of Baby Gem lettuce
- 1 tbsp chopped mint leaves
- 25g (1oz) butter
- 2 tbsp olive oil
- salt and pepper

Serves 4–6 | Vegetarian

1   Cook the peas with the chilli flakes in a saucepan of salted boiling water for 3–4 minutes, then drain. Meanwhile, chop the lettuce fairly finely and put it into a mixing bowl along with the mint.

2   Drain the peas and chilli in a fine colander. While still hot, add to the lettuce and mint. Add the butter and olive oil to the bowl and allow the butter to melt. Season with salt and pepper, toss and serve immediately.

Sugarsnaps & Chinese five spice

- 500g (1lb 2oz) sugarsnap peas
- 25g (1oz) butter
- 2 tbsp sesame oil
- 2 tsp Chinese five-spice powder
- juice of 1 lemon
- salt and pepper

Serves 4–6 | Vegetarian

1   Cook the sugarsnaps in a saucepan of salted boiling water for 2 minutes, then drain.

2   Melt the butter with the sesame oil in another saucepan, add the five-spice powder and cook over a medium heat for about 3–4 minutes, until the butter stops bubbling. Add the sugarsnaps and lemon juice and mix well. Season with salt and pepper and serve hot.

There are some lovely contrasts in this dish, especially the crunch of the sugarsnaps alongside the soft textures of the lamb stew. The couscous soaks up the liquids, and the cumin gets the taste buds going.

Sugarsnaps & couscous with lamb tagine

- 600g (1lb 5oz) couscous
- 500ml (18fl oz) water
- 500g (1lb 2oz) sugarsnap peas, roughly chopped

Tagine
- 2 tbsp olive oil
- 1kg (2lb 4oz) lean boneless lamb, such as leg, cut into 2cm (3/4in) cubes
- 1 white onion, diced
- 1 carrot, roughly chopped
- 4 garlic cloves, finely chopped
- 2 large tomatoes, skinned and roughly chopped
- juice of 1 lemon
- 350ml (12fl oz) Vegetable stock (see page 297)
- 200ml (7fl oz) medium-dry white wine
- 2 tbsp tomato purée
- 1 small bunch of flat leaf parsley, finely chopped
- 1 tsp toasted and crushed cumin seeds
- 1 cinnamon stick
- 1 small pinch of saffron threads
- salt and pepper

Serves 4–6

1   Heat the olive oil in a large saucepan, add the lamb and cook over a medium heat, stirring frequently, until lightly browned all over. Add the onion, carrot and garlic and cook gently for about 8 minutes, until tender, stirring occasionally.

2   Add the tomatoes and lemon juice to the pan and bring to a simmer. Continue simmering for 18–22 minutes, until the tomatoes begin to break down, stirring occasionally. Stir in the stock, wine and tomato purée, then add the parsley, cumin, cinnamon stick and 1 small pinch of saffron. Season to taste with salt and pepper. Bring to the boil, then reduce the heat and simmer, uncovered, for about 1 hour until the lamb is tender and the sauce is thickened, stirring frequently.

3   Meanwhile, put the couscous into a mixing bowl. Bring the water to the boil in a saucepan, pour over the couscous, then cover the bowl with a lid so that it seals the heat and steam in. Leave to cool. While the couscous is standing, cook the sugarsnap peas in a large saucepan of salted boiling water for 3 minutes, then drain. Remove the lid of the couscous bowl and use a fork to break up the couscous into a light, fluffy texture, then stir through the sugarsnaps. Remove the cinnamon stick from the lamb and serve with the couscous.

This recipe gives a lovely little nod towards Chinese cooking. Soy sauce, honey and peanuts work very well together, but you can use cashew nuts if you prefer.

Warm mangetout salad with honey & peanuts

- 500g (1lb 2oz) mangetout
- 25g (1oz) butter
- 2 tbsp olive oil
- 2 tsp clear honey
- 150g (5½oz) blanched raw peanuts
- 3 tsp soy sauce
- juice of 1 lemon
- salt and pepper

Serves 4–6 | Vegetarian

1   Cook the mangetout in a saucepan of salted boiling water for 2 minutes, then drain.

2   Melt the butter with the olive oil in another saucepan, then add the honey and cook over a medium heat for 3–4 minutes until the mixture starts bubbling. Add the peanuts, soy sauce and lemon juice and cook, stirring, for 1 minute before adding the mangetout. Mix well, then season with salt and pepper and serve hot.

Steaming in bamboo always adds a unique flavour to your cooking. I believe a bamboo steamer is an essential item in everyone's kitchen. The more layers it has the better.

Steamed buttered runner beans with lemon

– **500g (1lb 2oz) runner beans**
– **1 lemon**
– **50g (1¾oz) butter**
– **sea salt**

Serves 4–6 | Vegetarian

1   Trim the runner beans of their stringy sides – this is important, as perfectly decent runner beans become inedible if you don't remove their strings. Cut the beans into bite-sized pieces and lay them in layers in a bamboo steamer.

2   Set the steamer over a saucepan of hot water into which the juice of half the lemon has been squeezed. Steam the beans for 5–6 minutes, or until you are happy with their bite. Meanwhile, cut the remaining lemon half into slices.

3   Remove the lid and add a knob of butter and some lemon slices to each layer. Replace the lid, take to the table and serve hot.

Steamed leeks & spring onions

Trim and finely slice 4 young leeks and 1 bunch of spring onions. Add to a bamboo steamer and cook and serve as above.

I love the flourish of dropping a spoonful of homemade pesto into the middle of my soup bowl. My favoured approach is to taste the soup before I stir in the pesto, and then, as I begin to stir, I like to sample the flavour again before I go for the full stir-in. I love the golden colour of yellow French beans, but you can use green ones instead. You can also replace the pesto with my Classic tomato sauce (*see* page 211) if you prefer.

French bean minestrone with pesto

- 75ml (2¹/2fl oz) olive oil
- 1 white onion, cut into 1cm (¹/2in) dice
- 4 celery sticks, trimmed and cut into 1cm (¹/2in) dice
- 2 garlic cloves, finely chopped
- 200g (7oz) carrots, cut into 1cm (¹/2in) dice
- 150g (5¹/2oz) potato, peeled and cut into 1cm (¹/2in) dice
- 150g (5¹/2oz) baby turnips, peeled and cut into 1cm (¹/2in) dice
- 100ml (3¹/2fl oz) medium-dry white wine
- 1.5 litres (2³/4 pints) hot Vegetable stock (*see* page 297)
- 100g (3¹/2oz) dried fusilli pasta
- 100g (3¹/2oz) fresh peas, podded weight
- 500g (1lb 2oz) yellow French beans, trimmed and cut into 1cm (¹/2in) pieces
- 6 tsp Basil Pesto (*see* page 297)
- salt and pepper

Serves 6 | Vegetarian

1   Heat half the olive oil in a saucepan. Add the onion and celery and cook over a medium heat for 5 minutes, stirring occasionally. Add the garlic and cook for a further 3 minutes, stirring frequently.

2   Add the carrot, potato and turnip pieces to the pan with a pinch of salt and cook over a medium to high heat for 5 minutes, stirring frequently. Add the wine and cook for 5 minutes to allow the liquid to evaporate, then stir in the hot stock. Bring the soup to the boil and adjust the seasoning with salt and pepper. Reduce the heat and simmer for 10 minutes. Meanwhile, break the fusilli into 1cm pieces.

3   Add the broken pieces of fusilli to the soup and simmer for a further 10 minutes, then add the peas and French beans and simmer for another 4 minutes.

4   Ladle the soup into bowls, place a teaspoon of pesto in the centre of each serving and drizzle over the remaining olive oil.

This is such a cool dish to prepare, cook and serve, and your guests are sure to be impressed not only because it looks flashy but because it tastes fantastic.

Pan-fried French bean bundles with sesame seeds

- **450g (16 oz) fine French beans, trimmed**
- **ice cubes**
- **18 strips of pancetta**
- **3 tsp sesame seeds**
- **3 tbsp olive oil**
- **salt and pepper**

Serves 3–6

1   Prepare a bowl of very cold water and add some ice cubes. Put the beans in a large saucepan of salted boiling water and blanch for 2 minutes. Drain and then drop them into the iced water to help set their green colour.

2   When the beans are cold, drain and then lay them out on a tray. Dab them dry with kitchen paper. Lay the strips of pancetta vertically on a large chopping board with a 5cm gap between each strip. Gather up no more than 15 beans in your hand to form a bundle and place in the centre of the first strip of pancetta. Use the pancetta to roll the bundle of beans up so that it resembles a napkin with a napkin ring around it. Repeat with the remaining beans and pancetta.

3   Heat a large, dry frying pan over a medium to high heat, add the bean bundles, in batches, and cook until the fat starts to run from the pancetta, which will help with the cooking. If the pancetta is rather lean and gives off little fat, drizzle in 1–2 teaspoons of the olive oil. Cook the pancetta until golden brown, carefully turning the bundles to cook on both sides. Serve hot, sprinkled with the sesame seeds and drizzled with the olive oil.

In the early summer, when the beans are young and tender, just blanching them and then dressing them with a Dijon mustard vinaigrette and finely diced shallots tastes fantastic. I've added toasted almonds for a crunchy, creamy finish to this wonderful summery salad.

French beans with toasted almonds

- **600g (1lb 5oz) young tender French beans, trimmed**
- **3 large banana shallots**
- **300g (10¹/₂oz) flaked almonds**
- **75ml (2¹/₂fl oz) House dressing (*see* page 297)**
- **salt and pepper**

Serves 6 | Vegetarian

1   Wash the beans well in cold water, drain and then top and tail them. Add them to a large saucepan of salted boiling water and cook for 3 minutes until just tender but still with some bite to them. Drain, transfer to a tray and leave to cool at room temperature.

2   Meanwhile, finely dice the shallots, then add them to a mixing bowl. Heat a dry frying pan, add the flaked almonds and cook over a medium-high heat until they turn a light golden brown, shaking the pan frequently. Tip them on to a plate and leave them to cool before adding them to the diced shallots.

3   Add the dressing and the cooled beans to the bowl, mix well and serve.

The bright green of the okra and the purple tint of the aubergine really set each other off, and their delicate textures are enhanced with the crunch of the sesame seeds. It's a delicious feast for the senses.

Okra salad with sesame, honey & aubergine

- 600g (1lb 5oz) okra
- 1kg (2lb 4oz) aubergine
- 100ml olive oil
- 50g (1³/4oz) sesame seeds
- 100ml (3¹/2fl oz) runny honey
- salt and pepper

Serves 6 | Vegetarian

1   Wash the okra and chop off the tops, cut the okra into 3 cm long pieces and boil in salted water for 5 minutes. Drain and refresh then reserve at room temperature.

2   Cut the aubergine into 3cm (1¹/4in) cubes and then fry the aubergine in the olive oil. Once the aubergine is golden brown, tip it into a colander to drain off the oil then place in a large mixing bowl. Add the okra, honey and sesame seeds. Season and mix well, then serve at room temperature.

Basics

Shortcrust pastry

- 500g (1lb 2oz) plain flour
- 10g (¼ oz) salt
- 200g (7oz) cold butter, cut into small cubes
- 1 free-range egg, beaten
- 2 tbsp iced water

Makes about 700g (1lb 9oz) | Vegetarian

1 Put the flour and salt into a large mixing bowl, add the cubed butter and rub together with your fingertips until the mixture resembles breadcrumbs. Stir in the egg and iced water with a fork, then bring the mixture together with your hands to form a dough.

2 Return the dough to the bowl, cover with clingfilm and leave to rest in the refrigerator for 2 hours before using.

Cheese pastry

- 200g (7oz) plain flour
- 100g (3¼oz) cold butter, cut into small cubes
- 200g (7oz) Cheddar cheese, finely grated
- 4–5 tbsp iced water

Makes about 500g (1lb 2oz) | Vegetarian

1 Put the flour into a large mixing bowl, add the cubed butter and rub together with your fingertips until the mixture resembles breadcrumbs. Stir in the Cheddar and iced water with a fork, then bring the mixture together with your hands to form a dough.

2 Return the dough to the bowl, cover with clingfilm and leave to rest in the refrigerator for about 2 hours before using.

Pizza dough

- 350g (12oz) strong white bread flour, plus a little extra
- 1 tsp sea salt, crushed between your fingers
- 1 tsp caster sugar
- 1 tsp dried fast-action yeast
- 215ml (7½ fl oz) warm water

Makes 4 x 25cm (10in) base | Vegetarian

1 Put the flour into a warm place, such as an airing cupboard or a very low oven, for 30 minutes before use.

2 Sift the flour into a large mixing bowl and stir in the salt, sugar and yeast. Make a well in the centre and add the warm water. Using your first 2 fingers, mix in the flour, slowly building up to using your whole hand and then both hands to form the mixture into a ball of dough. If it seems a bit dry, add a little more water – the dough shouldn't stick to the back of your hand if you press down on it firmly but come away cleanly.

3 Place the dough on a lightly floured work surface and knead for 4 minutes, until it becomes elastic. To do this, push down on the centre of the dough with the palm of your hand, then fold it over towards you and give it a quarter turn. You might need to add a sprinkling of flour at this stage if your dough becomes sticky.

4 Return the dough to the mixing bowl, cover with a clean tea towel and leave in a warm place for 1½ hours, by which time the dough should have doubled in size; if it hasn't, leave for another 30 minutes.

5 Turn out the dough and give it a firm punch to release the air: this is known as 'knocking back'. Knead for another 2–3 minutes. Use as required.

Pasta dough

- 500g (1lb 2oz) '00' pasta flour, plus extra for dusting
- 5 free-range egg yolks
- 2 whole free-range eggs
- 2 tbsp olive oil

Makes about 600g (1lb 5oz) | Vegetarian

1 Tip the flour on to a dry work surface, make a well in the centre and add the egg yolks, whole eggs and olive oil. Using your hands, gradually mix the eggs into the flour until a dough forms.

2 Place the dough on the lightly floured work surface and knead for 15 minutes, until it begins to feel silky. Wrap the dough in clingfilm and place it in the refrigerator for at least 1½ hours while you prepare the filling.

Chicken stock

- 1 large boiling chicken
- 2 white onions, roughly chopped
- 2 large carrots, roughly chopped
- 2 celery sticks, roughly chopped
- 1 leek, roughly chopped
- 1 garlic bulb
- 2 bay leaves
- 2 thyme sprigs
- 1 tbsp white peppercorns
- 1 small dried red chilli
- 2 pinches of salt

Makes about 2 litres (3½ pints)

1 Put all the ingredients into a large saucepan, cover with cold water and bring to the boil. Skim off any white foam that rises to the surface and then add a further 2 litres (3½ pints) cold water. Return to the boil, then reduce to a simmer and continue simmering for 2 hours.

2 Strain the stock through a fine sieve and use as required. If not using straight away, leave to cool, then cover and keep in the refrigerator for up to 2 days, or freeze the stock for up to 3 months.

Vegetable stock

- 2 white Spanish onions, roughly chopped
- 2 carrots, roughly chopped
- 2 leeks, roughly chopped
- 1 garlic bulb
- 1 head of celery, trimmed
- 3 thyme sprigs
- 3 bay leaves
- 1 handful of parsley stalks
- 1 tbsp white peppercorns
- 1 tsp fennel seeds
- about 3 litres (5¼ pints) cold water

Makes about 3 litres (5¼ pints) | Vegetarian

1 Put all the ingredients into a large saucepan and bring to the boil. Skim off any white foam that rises to the surface, then reduce to a simmer and continue simmering for 20 minutes.

2 Strain the stock through a fine sieve and use as required. If not using straight away, leave to cool, then cover and keep in the refrigerator for up to 2 days, or freeze for up to 3 months.

Béchamel sauce

- 450ml (16fl oz) milk
- 1 bay leaf
- whole nutmeg, for grating
- 50g (1oz) butter
- 50g (1oz) plain flour

Makes about 450ml (16fl oz) | Vegetarian

1 Put the milk, bay leaf and a generous grating of nutmeg into a saucepan and heat until hot but without boiling.

2 Meanwhile, melt the butter in a medium saucepan, add the flour and stir well. Keep stirring over the heat and the mixture will start to bubble and lightly foam.

3 Add the milk a ladleful at a time (discarding the bay leaf), stirring constantly and watching carefully to avoid any lumps forming – a stiff balloon whisk can be helpful.

4 Once all the milk is used up, lower the heat and leave the sauce to simmer for a further 5 minutes to ensure that the flour is cooked, which gives the sauce a velvety texture. Use as required.

Tempura batter

- 600g (1lb 5oz) plain flour, plus extra for dusting
- 400ml (14fl oz) cold sparkling mineral water
- 200ml (7fl oz) olive oil

Makes about 1 litre (1¾ pints) | Vegetarian

1 Put the flour into a large mixing bowl and make a well in the centre. Add the sparkling water and oil to the well and, using a stiff balloon whisk, gradually blend in the flour until you have a smooth batter. For the silkiest result, set aside for at least an hour before using,

House dressing

- 100g (3½ oz) Dijon mustard
- 200ml (7fl oz) white wine vinegar
- 2 tsp salt
- 1 tsp pepper
- 300ml (½ pint) light olive oil

Makes about 600ml (1 pint) | Vegetarian

1 Put the mustard, vinegar, salt and pepper into a bowl and mix together well with a balloon whisk. Continue whisking and begin to add the oil in a slow, steady drizzle. You will see the mixture form an emulsion, becoming creamy but still retaining its pouring consistency.

2 When you have finished adding all the oil, check the seasoning and use as required. If not using straight away, cover and store in the refrigerator for up to 2 weeks.

Basil pesto

- 500g (1lb 2oz) basil leaves, as free of moisture as possible
- 100g (3½ oz) pine nuts
- 150g (5½ oz) Parmesan cheese, finely grated
- 1 small garlic clove, cut in half
- 200ml (7fl oz) olive oil
- salt

Makes about 350ml (12fl oz) | Vegetarian

1 Put all of the ingredients into a blender and blend until very smooth, but don't run the motor too long because the basil will start to heat up and discolour. Use as required. If not using straight away, cover and store in the refrigerator for up to 2 weeks.

Homemade mayonnaise

- 3 free-range egg yolks
- 1 tbsp Dijon mustard
- 2 tbsp white wine vinegar
- 1 tsp caster sugar
- 2 tsp salt
- pinch of pepper
- 500ml (18fl oz) vegetable oil
- 2 tbsp lemon juice

Makes about 600ml (1 pint) | Vegetarian

1 Put the egg yolks, mustard, vinegar, sugar, salt and pepper into a large metal bowl and mix well

with a balloon whisk. Place a folded damp tea towel under the bowl to hold it steady, and drizzle in the oil one-handed while continuing to whisk. If you prefer, simply ask someone to help you.

2 When you have whisked in three-quarters of the oil, add the lemon juice, then continue adding the rest of the oil. Check the seasoning and use the dressing as required. If not using straight away, cover and store in the refrigerator for up to 1 week.

Spicy mayonnaise

- 2 free-range egg yolks
- 2 tbsp white wine vinegar
- 1 large fresh red chilli, deseeded and chopped to a paste
- 1 tbsp Dijon mustard
- 250ml (9fl oz) light olive oil
- salt and pepper

Makes about 350ml (12fl oz) | Vegetarian

1 Put the egg yolks, vinegar, chilli and mustard into a large metal bowl and mix together well with a balloon whisk. Place a folded damp tea towel under the bowl to hold it steady as you whisk in the oil in a slow, steady drizzle (see above). The consistency should be smooth and pack a garlicky punch.

2 Check the seasoning and use as required. If not using straight away, cover and store in the refrigerator for up to 1 week.

Shallot dressing with herb vinegar

- 1 tbsp Dijon mustard
- 1 tsp caster sugar
- 50ml (2fl oz) herb vinegar
- 200ml (7fl oz) light olive oil
- 2 banana shallots, finely chopped
- 2 tbsp drained capers in vinegar, finely chopped
- 1 tbsp finely chopped tarragon
- salt and pepper

Makes about 250ml (9fl oz) | Vegetarian

1 Put the mustard, sugar and vinegar into a bowl and mix well with a balloon whisk.

2 Whisk in half the oil, add the chopped ingredients and continue adding the rest of the oil. Season with salt and pepper and use as required. If not using straight away, cover and store in the refrigerator for up to 2 weeks.

Sage butter

- 50g (1¾ oz) butter
- 12 sage leaves

Makes about 50ml (2fl oz) | Vegetarian

1 Heat the butter in a small saucepan until it starts to bubble. Add the sage leaves and fry over a medium heat for about 4 minutes, until they are lightly crispy. Serve immediately. Delicious drizzled over roasted squash or mash.

Apple jam

- 1.5kg (3lb 5oz) cooking apples, preferably all the same variety
- 1kg (2lb 4oz) caster sugar
- juice and finely grated rind of 2 unwaxed lemons

Makes 4 x small (500ml) jars | Vegetarian

1 Peel the apples, making sure to cut out any bruises, then core and slice the fruit very thinly. Pack the apple into a large, clean glass jar, place on a metal trivet in a saucepan and fill with enough boiling water to come up to the level of the apples. Leave to stew for 35–45 minutes, until quite tender.

2 Remove the jar with oven gloves and transfer the stewed apple to a clean saucepan. Add the sugar, lemon juice and lemon rind, bring to a simmer and continue simmering over a low-medium heat for 30 minutes, skimming off any white foam as it rises to the surface.

3 Meanwhile, put a saucer to chill in the refrigerator and sterilize 4 jam pots (follow step 3 of the method on page 180).

4 Test the jam by placing a spoonful of it on the chilled saucer and leaving in a cool place for a few minutes. Push the jam with your finger, and if the surface wrinkles, it is ready. If it doesn't show signs of setting, simmer for a further 5 minutes. Spoon the hot jam into the warm sterilized jar, and leave to cool before sealing tightly. Store in a cool, dark place for up to 3 months, or up to 6 months in the refrigerator. Once opened, refrigerate and use within 2 weeks.

Sauce soubise

- 50g (1¾oz) butter
- 4 white onions, finely chopped
- 150ml (¼ pint) Béchamel sauce (see page 297)
- 1 tbsp caster sugar
- 50ml (2fl oz) double cream
- salt and pepper

Makes about 250ml (9fl oz) | Vegetarian

1 Melt the butter in a heavy-based frying pan, add the onions and cook them over a very low heat for about 20 minutes so that they slowly stew in the butter, which creates a lovely sweet flavour.

2 Add the béchamel sauce and the sugar, then season with salt and pepper. Cook very gently for 30 minutes. Leave to cool slightly, then transfer to a blender and blend until very smooth, drizzling in the cream while you blend. Pour the sauce into a saucepan and reheat gently. Serve hot with baked potatoes or baked onions.

Gremolata

- 6 tbsp finely chopped flat leaf parsley
- 1 garlic clove, finely chopped
- finely grated rind of 2 unwaxed lemons
- 3 salted anchovy fillets, soaked in cold water for 30 minutes

Makes about 50ml (2fl oz)

1 Put the parsley, garlic and lemon rind into a small mixing bowl.

2 Drain the anchovies and chop them into the finest paste you can make. Add to the bowl and mix well with a spoon. Serve immediately. Delicious with baked potatoes or baked onions.

Garlic & herb bread

- 250g (9oz) butter, at room temperature
- 6 garlic cloves, finely chopped
- 1 shallot, finely chopped
- juice and finely grated rind of 1 unwaxed lemon
- 1 tbsp finely chopped flat leaf parsley
- 1 tbsp finely chopped chervil
- 1 tbsp finely chopped chives
- 1 French bread stick
- salt and pepper

Makes 1 loaf | Vegetarian

1 Preheat the oven to 180°C/fan 160°C/gas mark 4. Put the butter into a bowl, add the garlic, shallot, lemon rind and juice, herbs and salt and pepper and mix well using a stiff spatula.

2 Make cuts three-quarters of the way through the bread at 3cm (1¼in) intervals and spread the garlic and herb butter into each cut. Wrap the bread in foil and bake for 8 minutes. Remove from the oven, unwrap the bread and serve straight away.

Index

About the author

Arthur Potts Dawson is passionate about good food, eating well and making the most of what's fresh, local and seasonal. He was trained by the Roux Brothers, Rowley Leigh and Pierre Koffmann. He went on to be head chef for Ruth Rogers & Rose Gray at the River Café, the Soho House Group at Cecconi's, Jamie Oliver at Fifteen and Hugh Fearnley-Whittingstall at River Cottage HQ. He founded London eco-restaurants Acorn House and Water House for the Shoreditch Trust, and the Mrs Paisley's Lashings pop-ups with Jo Wood. Arthur has appeared on the BBC's *Market Kitchen*, in C4's *Food Fight* season and was featured on C4's *The People's Supermarket* documentary in 2011. Arthur lives in London and Somerset with his partner and two children, and he's working on his next restaurant. Check him out online on www.arthurpottsdawson.com.

Acknowledgements

Arthur Potts Dawson would like to thank...
My Family: Paloma Blanca, Aron Maze and Tuula Cherry for letting me spend so much time away from you and still loving me. My Mother, for carrying me. My Father Chris, for supporting me. My Dad for helping me. My Brothers: Julian, Demitri, Jon and Robert for your support and love – long live the brotherhood. Big up to Isaac, Ty, Neo, Thelonious, India, Brandon, Mali and Naja, you are the future of our family. Gill, Alexander, Albert & Eugenie. Mary, Alan, John & David. Sally, Louise, Rosie, Alice, Joshua, Jo, Anna, Nicola. To Mick & L'Wren for your inspiration. To Jade for your style, hi to Assisi and Amber. To Elizabeth, James & Anoushka, Georgia & Josh and Gabriel. To John & Lori Hillman for their guidance, to Francesca, John Jr, Laura, Carmen, Alex, Kike, Mercedes and Cherokee. To my Sifu, Steven Gerrard, always an inspiration in excellence, big shout to the dragon hall posse. To Helen Richards for keeping me real, to Kimberly Godbolt, big smiles. To the crew on The Cornishman, sailing out of Newlyn Harbour, keep safe, one and all. To Kate Wickes Bull for driving the revolution. To The People's Supermarket team, keep the faith. To Jo Wood, much love. To Jamie, Jesse, Leah, Jack & Maggie, Tyrone and the Mrs Paisleys Crew, Amy, Emily and Jake. Check out All the Queens Ravens, and Indigo Blue for future music. Thanks to the whole Octopus publishing team, Steph, Jo, Jonathan and David...... you rule.